You Can Do Anything You *Dynamically* Desire...Even What Seems Impossible!

" *A spire not only for what you think you're capable of achieving, but even more so for what you think you're incapable of achieving!*

"Be dedicated to developing dynamic desire, empowering yourself to consistently achieve even the seemingly impossible desires of your mind and heart.

"Do whatever it takes to set yourself up to create the life you yearn for... while enjoying the challenge and adventure of it all."

—The Publisher

Create a Richer, Happier, More Meaningful Life

The Power of Developing

Dynamic

Desire

Forge Ahead! Discover, Cultivate, Increase, and Sustain the Lifeblood of All Success

A
Gold Mine
of Life-Changing
Knowledge &
Wisdom

Bruce Garrabrandt

A *Possibility Press* Book

To my parents...Doris Horner Garrabrandt and James Bills Garrabrandt. Through the example of their lives they taught me the elements of success, happiness, and meaning.

Contents

Webster's Dictionary says... dy•nam•ic (di nam' ik), adj.

1. Pertaining to or characterized by energy or effective action; vigorously active or forceful; energetic: *the dynamic independent business owner.*

2. A basic or dynamic force, esp. one that motivates, affects development or stability, etc.

de•sire (di zī r̄), v.

1. To wish or long for; crave; want.

2. To express a wish to obtain; ask for; request.

3. A longing or craving, as for something that brings satisfaction or enjoyment; aspiration: *a desire for happiness and success.*

Therefore, you could say that Dynamic Desire means...

1. To be consistently energetic, constantly motivating yourself; taking vigorous effective action.

2. Doing whatever it takes to grow yourself, achieve your goals, and live the life you've been longing for in a way that reflects your purpose or calling: *the independent business owner who develops dynamic desire so he or she can become happier and more successful...continuing on the path of their purpose or calling.*

—Introduction—

Yes, You *Are* Gifted!

Unless you were born with a key in your back, don't expect anyone else to wind you up. Your best opportunity is NOW! So wind yourself up and diligently develop dynamic desire as you work toward your dreams and goals.

As a professional artist, I've exhibited my work in hundreds of juried shows over the past three decades. Many people ask, "Where did you go to art school?" I tell them I didn't! At the University of Delaware, I studied "pre-unemployment"—I was an English major.

I started drawing as a kid. Creating artwork good enough to frame and hang without embarrassment was a desire I longed to fulfill. Mom and Dad kept me well-stocked in paper and pencils. So I got started and, over time, taught myself to draw.

When I share this with people at art shows or seminars, they usually respond by saying, "Oh no, you have a gift. You were born with this talent." I smile and thank them, but I'm thinking, "Yes, I was born with this talent...*after a gestation period of about 10,000 hours!!!*"

8

In teaching myself to draw, I learned something more important than just how to be an artist. I discovered the truth about success. I once looked at successful people and saw only the success. "They were just lucky," I'd say to myself. "They were at the right place at the right time. They probably knew somebody or were born into wealth."

What most people *don't* see when they look at the successful, however, are the countless disappointments, rejections, and inevitable failures and frustrations encountered along the way. Many believe successful people are lucky or radically different from everyone else. But it's simply not true! It's often just a convenient way to justify a lack of accomplishment in a particular area in which they would like to succeed...a defensive stance or perhaps an excuse.

Let's face it, some people are lazy. It's easier to do just enough to get by, or maybe a little bit more. The path of mediocrity is always crowded. You'll certainly never be alone there, but neither will you ever be truly successful and happy.

Those who make it BIG understand we're all born with great potential; but without developing *dynamic desire* we won't amount to very much. Nothing is more powerful than someone with a strong sense of purpose and a passionate dynamic desire. He or she focuses on and takes action toward achieving their desire, *growing through* the disappointments, setbacks, negative responses, and discouragements until they achieve their goal...*then keep going to achieve more!*

Only *You* Can Change Your Life!

To accomplish much of anything, integrate these five elements into your daily life:

- Belief in Yourself
- A Sense of Purpose
- Action
- Discipline
- Perseverance

The Power of Developing Dynamic Desire can best be described as a motivational seminar in a book. An artist friend of mine who once held a corporate job told me he sat through a lot of such talks. "The speaker always fires you up," he said, "filling you with enthusiasm. When the talk is over, you leave the room feeling like you could conquer the world. Then you exit the building.... But if you don't take action before the week is over, you're back to your old lackluster routine."

Motivational seminars and books can't change your life. Only *you* can change your life! Take the excitement you feel and what you learn, and couple it with the power of developing dynamic desire. Speakers and authors do the talking and writing, but *you* must do the work! The great thing is... you're the one who will get the rewards for doing so.

We may look for shortcuts to the good life. We may say, "Someday when I win the lottery, I'll..." Forget it. You have a better chance of being struck by lightning while wearing a chicken suit than you do of winning the lottery.

You can be your own winning lottery ticket! "The whole secret of a successful life," said Henry Ford, "is to find out what it is one's destiny to do, and then do it." That may sound trite, but it's absolutely essential to understand and embrace...in order to apply and benefit from it. Do you believe we were created only to have our purpose here be so obscure that just a few people could ever figure it out?

We're on this planet to unlock our potential as human beings—to develop our passions and desires to such an extent that we turn them into talents and abilities! That takes dedication and hard and smart work. Nothing worthwhile comes otherwise. The only time you can expect quick progress is when your parachute doesn't open.

We're All Gifted—*the Gift Is Called Desire*

I tell people, "It took me 10,000 hours to learn how to draw." One kind woman said to me, "I could spend 10,000 hours drawing, but my pictures wouldn't look like yours. I'm not gifted like you are." Maybe not! Perhaps it would take her 15,000 or 20,000 hours to learn to draw—or maybe only 5,000. The truth is, she'll never know. The *desire* to draw isn't her gift. If it were, she'd be drawing and investing whatever time was necessary to learn the craft.

I can listen to a classical violinist play beautiful music, and say to myself, "It would be wonderful to play like that." But I'll never play, as I lack the desire to practice and get good at it. The desire to dedicate myself to the instrument simply isn't in me. Had I invested as much time playing the violin as I have invested in drawing since I was a boy—with the same degree of desire—I could be performing at Carnegie Hall today. But the desire to play the violin simply wasn't my gift.

As a teenager, though, whenever I walked through an art museum and saw paintings that moved me, I felt a hunger, a desire, to learn how that art was created. I studied the techniques—the use of color and light—and got excited by the prospects of improving my own work. I was filled with the *desire* to draw. That *desire* was and is my gift.

I remember sitting in the second grade, watching the teacher create colored chalk drawings on the blackboard to celebrate the change of seasons. We students were amazed to see those beautiful drawings appear before our eyes, but I wonder how many felt the desire to create their *own* drawings. How many said to themselves, "Whatever it takes, I will learn to do this"? At least one kid was thinking that—*me!*

We were all born gifted with the desire seeds to be, do, and have, and those, along with the new ones we discover as we journey through life, can be dynamically developed. Discover and dedicate yourself to yours and you can make them realities, using them as catalysts to create a richer, fuller, more meaningful, and rewarding life.

Throughout the book I refer to the subject of art, and introduce you to a number of professional artists. Since creating works of art is how I live my life, this is my primary frame of reference. But *The Power of Developing Dynamic Desire* is not a narrowly focused, how-to book for aspiring visual artists. Far from it! Whether you ever want to draw or paint or not isn't the issue. The issue is *your* desire—one of your most precious gifts.

To demonstrate the principles of success that can be applied to *any* professional or personal endeavor, I use famous artists, along with other well-known achievers, as examples of those who consistently strive for and attain excellence.

Webster's New World Dictionary defines artist as: "(1) a person skilled in any of the fine arts; (2) a person who does anything very well, with imagination and a feeling for form, effect, etc." This second definition is the core of *The Power of Developing Dynamic Desire* and it will define *you*...when you apply the five key elements of success to your own endeavors.

"But I'm Only *One* Person!"—*That's Where It All Starts*

A powerful fact of life is that your accomplishments can be much greater than you may now envision. Charles Kettering, founder of General Motors, said, "It is amazing what ordinary people can do if they set out without preconceived notions." Everyone is ordinary, but some of us do extraordinary things; that's all. Unfortunately, most of us grossly undervalue our potential. "But I'm only *one* person!" we may say.

Teresa, an artist friend, creates primitive folk art. I love her response to anyone who complains, "But I'm only one person!" "Oh really?" she says. "Well, how many people was Thomas Jefferson? How about Eleanor Roosevelt? And what about Mother Teresa?"

"But I'm only one person!" is just a convenient excuse for copping-out, for doing nothing, which is absolutely refuted in any biography of note. Each of us has unique contributions to make. It's up to us to do what is ours to do. No matter our circumstances, we're capable of growing into the person we were meant to be. To do so requires that we begin by developing dynamic desire. That's what this book is all about.

No one is trapped in some clear polymer—like a seahorse in a paperweight. We *can* better ourselves, and in the process be more, do more, and have more. Every day we *could* see the awakening of more of our potential. But most of us just sleepwalk through life. Scratch the surface of some people and you'll only find more surface! How sad.

Unfortunately, few of us do more than care for the surface of our lives. Like thin strips of sod laid over hard clay, we seldom take root and grow deeply.

In many cases, people are just getting by, melding into the unhappy masses. If, according to the familiar saying, "All the world's a stage," why do so many settle for just being a part of the audience, watching others enjoying success? Remember, life is not a spectator sport. Get in the game and participate! Follow your heart's desires. Make your dreams come true, and create a masterpiece of your life.

Keep in mind as Henry Wadsworth Longfellow said, "Lives of the great men [and women] all remind us that we can make our lives sublime; and in departing, leave behind us footprints on the sands of time."

Life serves us a wonderful hot fudge sundae, but few come anywhere near to enjoying it in totality. Most never get beyond the whipped-cream topping, while some spend their time searching for a napkin to polish the spoon.

The Power of Developing Dynamic Desire is designed to help you enjoy more of your sundae. Now is the time to "dig in," commit to your desire, develop it dynamically, and enjoy the process.

""*F*ew men or women during their lifetime come anywhere near exhausting the resources dwelling within them. There are deep wells of strength that are never used."*

—Admiral Richard E. Byrd

Chapter 1
Believe in Yourself

"There are admirable potentialities in every human being. Believe in your own strength. Learn to repeat endlessly to yourself: 'It all depends on me.'" —André Gide

Suppose I ask you to sum up, in one sentence, your personal philosophy of life. Could you do it? What would you say? Well, let me give you mine: No matter what you've accomplished in life so far, you are still mostly potential. Successful people know this. They feel it in their bones. Many have said it better than I.

Admiral Richard E. Byrd, the polar explorer, believed that, "Few men or women during their lifetime come anywhere near exhausting the resources dwelling within them. There are deep wells of strength that are never used."

Psychologist William James said, "Compared to what we could be, many of us are only half awake."

The potential you need to be successful is right inside your mind and heart. Within you lies the power to become the person you want to be—unless, of course, you want to be someone else!

15

That's the power and the wonder of life. You have, between your ears and in your heart, what it takes to be successful at whatever you desire to do. Your foundation for success begins with your heartfelt desire and intention—not so-called gifts and talents. From that you can springboard to build a more successful life, whatever that is for you.

Do you recognize these statements?

"Know thyself."

"If you have faith, as a mustard seed, nothing shall be impossible to you."

"Neglect not the gift that is in thee."

Make No Mistake About It—*You Were Born to Succeed*

When life asks us to audition and says, "Show us what you can do!" many position themselves both on stage and in the audience. All too often, a timid performer stands in the spotlight only to be shouted down by their own-heckling-self seated in the front row.

"No life has ever been lived," said Mark Twain, "which was not a failure in the secret judgment of the person who lived it."

Unfortunately, far too many tend to see themselves, deep down, as damaged goods, fit only for the discount bin of life. Most criticize and undervalue themselves in ways their worst enemies would never even dream of. If others saw us as many of us see ourselves, their criticisms would keep us by ourselves, indoors, with the shades pulled down.

Not many would choose themselves for a best friend. How sad is that? After all, you've got yourself for a lifetime! No matter where you go, you take yourself along for the ride. So you might as well be your own best friend and best self!

Two elderly women visited my booth at one of my art shows, striking up a conversation with me about creativity.

"I have no talents," one lamented.

"Oh, I'm sure you do," I said.

"No," she insisted, "I can't do anything well."

"How have you survived this long?" I asked playfully.

"I don't know," she laughed.

"Before you leave my booth, would you tell me three qualities you like about yourself?" I asked.

She paused for a moment and said, "I don't know. I've never thought about that." She then turned to her friend and asked, "What do I like about myself?"

"No fair asking someone else," I said. "I want to hear *your* answers."

"Well," she said with a smile, "let me walk around the show, and I'll stop back with my answers."

She never returned.

Surveys have shown that most of us say we believe in God, yet too few people choose to believe in themselves. To my mind, that's like praising an architect and then being afraid to walk inside one of his or her buildings! We need to be appreciative of our own and others' potential. Each of us was born for a reason.

"What lies behind us and what lies before us are tiny matters," wrote Emerson, "compared to what lies within us." You have a vast reservoir of power available to you. Look no further than yourself to find it. That's part of what having faith is all about. Do you trust and know that you were born to live a meaningful life? If not, would you be willing to?

Thoughts Create Feelings...*Feelings Don't Just Happen!*

The human brain is a vast source of power. As it says in Proverbs, "As a man thinketh in his heart, so is he." What you think determines the way you feel and act. You can do nothing without first thinking about it. If you only rock back and forth, and stare into the middle distance, even these simple actions first require thought.

We're all creatures of habit, establishing certain routines for ourselves. Admittedly, routine is comfortable and gives our lives a sense of order. Look at the daily rituals of your life and examine the patterns of thinking you've formed. Routine actions are the products of such thoughts, and these thoughts and actions create how you perceive yourself.

Do you see yourself as inadequate? Listen to the messages you give yourself. Begin to observe how your thoughts keep you from venturing beyond what is safe and familiar. The very act of recognizing disempowering thoughts enables you to gain control over them. Do you ever say to yourself...

- "I'm set in my ways"?
- "I'm too old to change"?
- "I can't do that"?
- "I will fail"? or
- "It won't work"?

If so, can you understand how saying these things could be hindering your success?

These routine thought patterns are formed to keep our lives predictable and safe—safe, but probably sorry. Our doubts and disclaimers are the silk we spin into protective cocoons. They help us avoid facing the risks and responsibilities of change but also keep us from ever having the rewards.

You can never hit your head against the ceiling of your potential. Your thinking and actions determine the degree to which you will fulfill your potential. The great news is that your mind is infinitely more powerful than any negative thoughts to which it may be exposed, and by developing your dynamic desire you can do anything you set you mind to.

We're often guided by our emotions, yet may fail to understand that every feeling is first brought on by a thought. But many frequently take the opposite view: "I feel inadequate, so I don't think I can succeed." But feelings don't dictate thoughts. Thoughts come first, triggering our feelings, whether they're negative or positive.

Think you are inadequate and feelings of inadequacy will follow on the heels of that negative, disempowering thought. If you dance with negativity, your thoughts have led you there. So dance and lead with empowering positivity. Think positive and you'll feel and act positive!

Unleash the Power of Developing *Dynamic* Desire

My home is over 160 years old, built by a prosperous farmer named Samuel Watts. He erected the house as much for his grandchildren as he did for himself.

Most people weren't as mobile in those days. Often they were born, lived, and died in the same house; so homes were built to last. In our basement are large, wooden joists which span the width of the house, providing strong structural support. Their function is vital to the integrity and survival of the dwelling.

Recognize the reality of that same kind of support inside yourself. You are created with strong joists which provide the material strength to weather life's disappointments, stresses, and setbacks. Right thinking calls on their strength. Have faith that they're part of your internal structure.

Believe in yourself. Know that you're made to meet and conquer any challenges or obstacles that come your way. You're built for success, and you need to remain aware of your strong joists. Know them firmly in your mind, feel them strongly in your heart...and *nothing* can stop you.

Let's face it. Many ask where we came from and why we're here. We know the people we love will die—including ourselves—and seemingly all too soon. No wonder many of us are so insecure and unsure of ourselves, but we needn't be. Since life is so short, adopt a sense of urgency in making the most of it...starting right NOW!

Have a trusting attitude in believing your life is full of purpose and that you possess enormous, untapped potential. Know your life can become rich with meaning as you contribute to some greater good, believing you can become prosperous in the process.

You were born with the freedom of choice. You can choose to be fearful and unsure, or you can choose to be confident, successful, and fulfilled. It's all a matter of faith. Your land of possibilities is wide open unless you bring along the fencings and a post-hole digger to fence yourself in.

You may recognize the definition of faith as, "The substance of things hoped for, the evidence of things not seen." Everything good stems from faith. With faith in yourself in moving forward, every day becomes an adventure as you continue stretching, growing, and experiencing new things.

Have faith and trust that you were designed to play a positive role in the world—that you're here to succeed. You cannot become a success without the love and support of yourself.

Unfortunately, few people commit to themselves and their desire…most only "cohabitate" with themselves. Some even act as if they'd prefer a separation from themselves!

When we commit to ourselves and our heartfelt desire with faith, we gain an inner peace which accompanies us on our journey. Though we may encounter rocky periods of disappointment and failure along the way, thoughts that lead to feelings of serenity will help to smooth our road and keep us moving forward at a steady, confident pace.

We all know people who, even in times of great pressure and stress, maintain an unruffled attitude. Chaos swirls around them in the form of unforeseen challenges, irate customers, clients, coworkers, or associates, phones constantly ringing and vibrating, impossible deadlines, and texts and emails piling up. Yet these people are the calm in the center of the storm.

"Quiet minds cannot be perplexed or frightened," said Robert Louis Stevenson, "but go on in fortune or misfortune at their own private pace, like a clock ticking during a thunderstorm." Just reading that gives you a peaceful feeling, doesn't it?

Sometimes life dares us to find meaning in our existence. This is when our faith is truly defined. People of faith possess the will to carry on when everything looks bleak. They trust and know that they are alive for a purpose.

Recognize that you come equipped with sturdy, internal joists. The strength they provide is beyond dispute. People of courage are, and always have been, people of faith. They believe themselves to be part of something richer and deeper than themselves.

The Miracle of You

We oftentimes fail to appreciate how miraculous life is because we're right smack in the middle of it. The fact is: You *are* miraculous! Your life *is* special. Anthropologist Margaret Mead said, "You are unique—just like everyone else." Perhaps her point was to caution us not to let our egos inflate. However, I prefer to interpret her words as a statement about the marvelous nature of human beings.

Each of us is endowed with a unique gift called desire, and the potential to be an instrument for greater good. Believe this, as well as in yourself, while making personal development a part of the mission of your life.

Personal development and being the best we can be, and then bettering it…that's our job. Some of us get to the job early and stay late. Some live for vacations and personal days. Others seem to be always on break or out to lunch.

The dawn of each new day is to be in all our hearts, as well as on the horizon. What skills can we develop to help us best serve others? "To be of use in the world," said Hans Christian Andersen, "is the only way to happiness."

Many people say to me, "But I'm not good at anything. I wasn't born with any talent." Well, no one I know of was born with anything but a talent for crying and creating dirty diapers. To become really good at anything else, you must work at it. No one is born with fully developed, innate abilities, but everyone is born with an innate potential that can only be cultivated by developing the power of dynamic desire. This is an essential belief if you are to be successful at anything in life.

Mentally embrace the power of positive knowing. Begin with a commitment to the fact that you're here to be a creative, productive, successful human being. Accept that everyone has periods of self-doubt, when positive thinking may feel like a meaningless exercise.

What sustains you at such times is the underlying knowledge that, despite inevitable failures, which indicate that you are in training...a work in progress...you're destined to triumph by developing dynamic desire, as well as applying persistent effort, imagination, and dedication to personal growth. Know and consistently apply these truths from the core of your being, and successful living will become your reality.

Perhaps your parents failed to inspire, encourage, and challenge you or didn't give proper guidance. Maybe none of your teachers believed in you enough to challenge and empower you to reach greater heights, perhaps resulting in school years that may have been boring for you. Regardless, there must be some worthwhile reason for your heart to keep beating and your brain to keep working, or you wouldn't still be here.

When you accept and understand, with gratitude, the gift of your precious life and your innate potential, that's reason enough to dedicate yourself to excellence. Your best defense against defeat is gratitude in the present moment. Since you obviously have a pulse—be grateful; you're full of potential!

We're not created with a predestination to fail. We're designed to handle stumbles and falls with the ability to regain our balance, stand up again, dust ourselves off, and move forward. You learned this a long time ago, or you'd still be crawling around on the floor on your hands and knees. What you discovered when you were a toddler is a lesson to be carried throughout life. It's okay to fall down now and then; but you were built to stand up and get to wherever you want to go. Your creative possibilities become virtually infinite once you recognize that you have great potential.

Are you nearsighted to the majesty whirling around you? As you acquire a broader view, you can expand your life and enrich its meaning. We are given both the power to reason and the power to believe. Logic and faith are mighty tools. The challenge may be to discern when to use each.

If you feel yourself drowning in a seemingly meaningless life, just clinging to reason can't save you. Only by letting go, which is an act of faith, will you find yourself floating, buoyed by an inner confidence and calm, toward a bountiful shore.

Philosopher John Stuart Mill said, "One person with belief is equal to a force of 99 who have only interests."

Frank Lloyd Wright, the great architect, told us, "The thing always happens that you believe in, and the belief in a thing makes it happen."

To believe that you've been given no gifts is to say you were created without a purpose. I don't accept that. How about you? We're all gifted with desires and interests, along with the ability to choose an appropriate course of action, believing it will develop and lead us to their realization.

Turn inward. See the miracle that you are and recognize your current and potential strengths. Set a goal that'll help you best utilize your desire and begin taking steps toward achieving it. Think. Plan. Act. We're here to dream and do. You've been put on this earth for a reason. Whether or not you choose to determine what it is and focus on it is another matter.

If you're not currently a self-starter...become one! Life will rarely leave you feeling burned out once you learn how to light your own fire and keep it roaring. It's your responsibility to pursue excellence—no one can do it for you. You owe it to yourself, your family, and your fellow human beings to be the best you can be...then better it!

Potential was given to you at birth with the supporting structure in place. A great power lies within you, and you are your own safety net. Have faith in yourself. "As soon as you trust yourself," said poet Goethe, "you will know how to live."

Desire Confirms the Certainty of Unrealized Potential

When Walt Disney first made the rounds in Hollywood, peddling his desire to make a talking mouse a "movie star," studio executives dismissed it as far-fetched and unworkable. No one took his idea seriously.

Undaunted, young Disney took it upon himself to create and market the dream he called "Mickey." Determined to succeed, he refused to let any negative opinions undermine his confidence. Walt believed in himself and the eventual reality of his dream as he had been developing dynamic desire. The results of his unshakable optimism survive and thrive, stronger than ever, half a century after his death.

Whenever he got a new idea, a desire, Disney said he asked 20 people what they thought of it. If they were unanimous in their disapproval, he'd go full speed ahead with it! Disney showed us how faith and trust can make for lasting power. When you sufficiently cultivate, sustain, and develop your desire it can propel you to wherever you want to go.

Your potential is a vast, unexplored continent. Be courageous; venture into it. If you foolishly ignore a large part of it, you won't accomplish what was in your heart and on your mind to do. Claim your potential, commit to it, and keep moving forward. Develop the dynamic desire, as well as the faith, trust, and optimism, to do whatever it takes to go for it.

Only You Can Create Your Own World

In a real sense, you create your own world. If you see it through cynical eyes, your life can become a pointless, seemingly endless struggle—a predatory affair in which narrow, selfish motives direct human behavior and strangers are viewed with suspicion.

But when you see the world through the eyes of a successful person, it becomes a wonderful place where the loving gift of dynamic desire has been developed. You'll find countless examples of warm, friendly people whose conduct enriches the lives of others, whose desires ennoble and dignify all of us.

People with a dynamic desire perspective create a world of purpose and deep meaning. For them, life becomes a beautiful adventure, a precious opportunity to develop and express their gifts and abilities in positive, fulfilling ways, benefiting themselves and others.

Cruel and brutal, or loving and generous, the kind of world you see will determine the quality of people and experiences which fill your life. In either case, your expectations will be fulfilled.

Stop Comparing Yourself to Others

A man looked at my drawings at one of my art shows and said, "You certainly were given a gift—a wonderful talent."

"Thank you," I said, "but the gift wasn't talent. It was the *desire* to draw. I'm self-taught."

"I think you have to possess the talent to begin with," he told me. "A kid I was friends with in grade school used to make drawings of buildings. They were quite beautiful. I was jealous because it came so easily to him. I couldn't possibly draw as well as he did. I tried, but it was frustrating for me, so I gave up.

"Now I just admire other artists' works and hang them on my walls. Today, my artist friend is a successful architect. Others could study and practice forever, but never come close to being as good an architect as he is. No matter what they do, they'll always be average."

"Maybe so," I told him, "but we're not here to become the best that *someone else* can be. We must grow into the best that *we* can be, and then improve on that best. It's as simple as that!"

Now, you could say to me, "That sounds very nice, but not everyone can be great." But you'd be wrong. We're all born with the seed of greatness which must be nurtured in order to grow and become what it was created to be. You may never become famous, but you can become great! All "fame" means is that more people know about your greatness. Besides which, fame is fleeting.

I may never be a famous artist, but I'm always inspired by the Great Masters. I marvel at the work of colored pencil artists whose productivity and recognition outdistance mine. So what? I love to draw, and I've persevered long enough to become somewhat accomplished. As Mother Teresa said... "It's not how much we do, but how much love we do it with."

Having developed a degree of expertise in my field, I'm personally free and able to live quite well by doing what I enjoy. That, in my mind, is success. I don't have to be the richest or most well known, compared to other artists, at what I do. Don't waste any time comparing yourself to others in your field either. We long to soar like eagles, forgetting that sparrows, too, enjoy flying. They are being the best they can possibly be.

Unlike the sparrow, however, you and I can all be better than we currently are. We can all become eagles. We all have room for growth. You can never hit your head against the ceiling of your potential.

Furthermore, as Harvey C. Fruehauf said, "There's no ceiling on effort." What an exciting fact of life! You can continue the joy of overcoming challenges by dynamically developing the gift of your desire. This empowers you to gain the skills that enable you to become who you were meant to be. You can then more effectively go for fulfilling your potential...every day for the rest of your life.

Everyone encounters obstacles between themselves and their desire, most using them as excuses, causing them to stay stuck. Successful people, however, overcome their obstacles by stretching and growing rather than simply settling for the status quo. The successful choose to deal with and overcome their challenges with the driving force of their dynamic desire, doing so in a positive, possibility thinking way.

Adversity, like a strong competitor when met and dealt with, can bring unexpected abilities out of us that can be astonishing. The obstacles you overcome are like chisels, slowly sculpting you into a work of art.

Admire other people's levels of accomplishment, but don't be intimated or awed by them. Otherwise, you may rob yourself of the opportunity to become more than you ever dreamed possible. Remember, there's always someone who has more than you do. Rather than comparing ourselves to others and what they are, have, and do, compare what we have and where we are now to what and where we could be.

Remember those kids in high school who never had to study? (You may have been one of them!) Good grades seemed to come effortlessly. More than once I sat sweating over essay test questions while the student next to me had already turned in his or her blue (test) book. I, in no way, could have competed with that student's speed of learning and recall. So what?

Would it have been better if I had torn up my test book and left the classroom? If learning a subject takes you five times longer than it does for someone else, so what? As long as you eventually master the material and keep moving forward, isn't that what matters most?

I once knew a man, we'll call him Fred, who continually compared himself to others. He was caught in the comparison trap. Fred measured his success strictly in material terms.

He liked to view himself as doing better and having more than those around him. It wasn't enough for Fred that he owned a nice house. The fact that most of his friends still lived in apartments and condos made him feel personally superior to them.

Fred's appreciation for what he owned was always predicated on how well it stacked up against what others possessed. Unfortunately, his choosing to compare determined his level of satisfaction. He involved himself in a constant, unrelenting game of one-upmanship.

On several occasions, Fred talked about an elderly relative. When this person died, he would inherit his big old house in the mountains. Rather than enjoying his current home, Fred and his wife mentally had this man dead and buried and were talking about what they'd do with the place. They were practically picking out furniture and choosing curtains.

How unfortunate that Fred based his happiness on what he owned, and obsessed over how his things ranked with others' possessions. He'll be forever running a race he cannot win, scrambling in vain to catch up to people who have more. Rather than living in competition with friends, neighbors, associates, and coworkers, Fred...and those like him...would do well to step back and look with heartfelt gratitude upon their most valuable possession: the gift of life itself.

Instead of concerning ourselves with how well *others* are doing, we all need to be grateful for what we have and ask ourselves, "How can I become a better person?" As a by-product of our growth and greater contributions, we'll be able to enjoy the fruits of our labor.

Life offers so much more to those who drop out of the "rat race" and the "comparison trap," and find the value in each moment. When we compete with ourselves through our own personal growth—and strive to realize more of our inner capabilities—we discover how little time remains for egotistical competition with anyone else.

Rediscover Your Sense of Wonder

"It takes a long time to become young," said Pablo Picasso. He understood well how the root of our creativity is founded in our sense of wonder.

"What do you want to be when you grow up?" adults asked us when we were kids. "As powerful as I am now," could have been our answer. Young children are full of creative power. Their imaginations are rich with fanciful ideas and the desire to play and learn. Unfortunately, those qualities are often squelched during our school years by adults who claim they know better.

Robert Fulghum, bestselling author of *All I Really Need to Know I Learned in Kindergarten*, is often invited to speak at schools, usually to kindergarten and college-level classes. He's always struck by the difference in self-confidence between the two groups.

For example, Fulghum asks a roomful of five-year-olds, "How many of you can sing?" All hands go up. He asks, "How many of you can draw?" Everyone can draw. "How many can dance?" They all can. "How many can act?" All hands wave eagerly.

Fulghum also asks these same questions when speaking to college students. Unfortunately, he sees relatively few hands raised in positive response, and those who *do* respond are usually timid about it.

Fulghum wonders what happened to the desire and boundless enthusiasm of these former five-year-olds. Sadly, he hears students talk about their limitations, lack of confidence, and circumstances.

Large classrooms of students are generally not conducive to the development of individuality—depending, to some extent, of course, on the teacher or professor. Following instructions and learning by rote are usually emphasized over creativity and imaginative participation. Reading, writing, and arithmetic are essential elements of a solid education, but they aren't enough for realizing one's potential. Some even say that all they learned in school was how to pass tests.

If we are to understand our unique gift of desire, we need to first reclaim the sense of wonder about life and its marvelous possibilities that we had as children. Such awe stimulates creative thinking and open-mindedness, which can guide us to greater achievement.

Commitment to keeping your creative spirit alive provides you with opportunities daily to experience, once again, all the magic of childhood... this time without getting chicken pox.

Those who are stuck in the same old monotonous routines have made their minds virtual monuments—their lives reflecting rigid, regimented, close-minded, boring patterns of thinking. Those who are excited about life and constantly exploring and pushing for their potential have made their minds jungle gyms for imagination. How about you?

One Father's Legacy

When children have someone nurturing their sense of wonder, it can have a powerful, positive effect that sets them up for a life of accomplishment.

While a student at the University of Delaware, I made regular pilgrimages to the Brandywine River Museum in Chadds Ford, Pennsylvania. There I found inspiration in the work of America's foremost artistic family—the Wyeths. N. C. Wyeth was celebrated for his illustrations of literary classics. But his greatest artistic achievement was the desire for creative spirit that he imparted to his children.

A Smithsonian program for public TV profiled the Wyeth family. Interviews with N. C.'s children, by then senior citizens, revealed the profound impact their father's childlike approach to life had had on them.

Nat, the eldest son, was a successful engineer; holding 23 patents. Among his many inventions was the plastic soda bottle. His sister Ann became an accomplished musician and composer. Siblings Carolyn, Henriette, and Andrew followed in their father's artistic footsteps.

Now, some may say all there talents were in their genes. But don't believe it. What made the difference in their lives was how N.C. taught his children to observe the world. He understood that life only exhilarates those who take big, spontaneous gulps of it.

"Soak it all up," he advised them. "Be like a sponge." He was determined to infuse his children with a lifelong creative spirit and sense of wonder, and he certainly succeeded in doing so. Writer David McCullough described it as "growing up in a magical household where being creative and being alive were one and the same thing."

N.C. was a dedicated, compassionate father. He never talked down to his children—he treated them as peers. "Keep alive to everything and carry it with you," he told them. "When you are open to all of life, you're in a schoolroom."

Play was an essential component of the Wyeth household. The family performed elaborate skits and often filmed these amateur productions as home movies. N.C. brought home piles of paper, pencils, and paints for his kids.

"Use plenty of materials," he instructed; "plenty of paint." The man overflowed with passion for life. He savored it in all of its details. He exposed his children to a world of excellent music, excellent books, and excellent art. He taught them how to see, hear, and think expansively. "Do everything in a big way!" was his fatherly advice.

If we wade through life, we'll be happy only up to our shins. To be drenched with delight, we must live deeply. N.C. Wyeth knew this and lived it every day.

He once took his family to see the film *Mutiny on the Bounty*. When the movie ended, he quickly herded his children into the lobby to observe the audience as these people exited the theater. "Look at all those dull faces," he said. He warned them about the great limitation of film—it offers moviegoers no interaction of imagination. It's a passive endeavor of watching other people live their lives—rather than fully living our own. It's often a temporary escape to alleviate the boredom of the average person's life.

The Smithsonian's biography of the Wyeths concludes with excerpts from one of N.C.'s many letters. The artist's words reflect his personal life philosophy, a great lesson in how to live creatively. We would all do quite well to adopt it for ourselves:

> "My imagination is on fire. The universe towers in my mind a great, overpowering mystery. The significance of the tiniest speck of bark on the pine tree assumes the proportions of the infinite sky. My brain almost bursts with the effort to really appreciate the meaning of life, of existence. I ardently promise, with all my soul, to do my best to make my short life of use, to add an infinitesimal light to the world."

Creative vision isn't a matter of being born with the right genetics. It comes when we rediscover that five-year-old child within, and proclaim to the world, "Yes, I can do that!"

I'm of average intelligence, and you may be too. That's fine. I don't let it hold me back, and you needn't either. Why? Even with average intelligence I have more potential than I can possibly realize in my lifetime, and so do you.

So constantly grow and expand your horizons. Develop your deepest desire, which is truly your greatest challenge. Creatively better your best; that's where you'll find your most valuable contribution, as well as your greatest joy.

What About Self-Esteem?

Many people fail and are unhappy due to their poor self-esteem—lacking respect for themselves. I listen to talk radio when I'm drawing and hear people frequently saying things like this: "I grew up in a dysfunctional family. I was never made to feel important. Because of the way I was treated in the past, I don't feel good about myself."

This may well be true, but it shouldn't be held up as a banner that's waved in hopes of getting sympathy, or used as an excuse to prevent you from growing and moving forward. We all hurt in some way—we've all had our share of challenges. Don't kid yourself that you're the only one with hurdles to leap over. As my publisher says to complainers, "I'm glad I'm not the only one with problems!"

Sometimes people erroneously forever link self-esteem to family history. But I especially like Lincoln's opinion of obsession with ancestry: "I'm less concerned with what my grandfather did than in what his grandson will do."

Problems arise if we allow our self-esteem to be dependent upon circumstances outside ourselves, which only leaves us totally vulnerable to exterior forces. Take this false idea of self-esteem and throw it out the window, along with all the negative messages you may have given yourself.

You alone are responsible for developing your own healthy self-esteem; no one else can bestow it upon you. Others can encourage you, but you're the only one with the power to better yourself and thereby raise your self-esteem. It's up to you to desire and create the positive circumstances that will contribute to your creating a more fulfilling life.

To quote my publisher again, "Do you respect yourself enough—have you grown your self-esteem enough—to do whatever it takes to live the life you want?"

Self-esteem is intertwined with self-belief, which is a paycheck earned through rigorous employment of your abilities in reaching for your potential. Anyone who's waiting for handouts has another thing coming. Handouts don't build self-esteem and self-belief—they reinforce weakness.

If you expect others to create a great life for you, you'll be waiting forever. It just isn't going to happen! It's your responsibility, and yours alone, to nurture and constantly develop your dynamic desire to where it bolsters the self-esteem and self-belief you need to create a great life...as *you* define it.

Are You Safe and Secure?

In the "Parade of Life," people often settle for being the crepe paper on a poorly constructed float. Don't be one of them.

What do you dream of being, doing, and having? Write a list of any reasons why you think you'll probably never achieve your dream. Then throw the list away! Stop making excuses. Life offers us the run of the mansion, but our comfort zone is usually inside the broom closet.

Why aren't most people vigorously pursuing their dreams? First of all, they feel safe in their daily routines, opting for so-called security. They're letting themselves be held hostage by it. But, as General Douglas MacArthur warned, "There is no security; there is only opportunity." As humorist James Thurber said, "There's no safety in numbers, or in anything else."

If you pause amid the business of your life to seek out one, tiny corner of safety and security, you're only kidding yourself. Don't look for a safety net in life. Your life is an opportunity. It's better not to be safe and sorry. Become a sensible risk-taker. Begin making plans to become greater than you are.

To get more out of life, get more out of yourself. It's a fundamental fact that, as long as you continue to have brainwave activity, you can do more. You're always unfinished business—a work in progress. Your growth needs to remain number one on your to-do list. The more you grow, the more you can succeed.

Security yawns and closes its eyes to possibility. The moment you make security your primary goal in life, you begin to die. To settle for a comfortable routine is like doing all of your grocery shopping at a convenience store. You'll pay an exorbitant price for what you purchase there. The cost in life is your precious potential.

Look around. Most people, perhaps unknowingly, choose to shut down their desires and remain unfulfilled. They conform to the conventional and blend in with the masses. Why does Mediocrity sit and scratch itself on Mount Untapped Potential? Because it's easier! We can opt for mediocrity in life and still have our basic needs met. We can get food, shelter, and clothing without pushing ourselves very hard. But is that how you want to live? Is that what you want your life to stand for? That's no dream.

Though we're all meant to be in the game, the sidelines are full of people out of uniform, passively sitting in the bleachers. "I do enough to get by" seems to be their personal life slogan. Two other mottoes are "Don't make waves," and "Just go with the flow."

We're not here to be average. Average is the top of the bottom and the bottom of the top. It's really nowhere. We were created to excel and succeed. In time, "the path of least resistance" often becomes heavily rutted with boredom, dissatisfaction, and unhappiness...even despair.

The creative spirit of desire is built into us. To ignore it in favor of comfort and conventional routine is to squander one of life's greatest gifts. Push out of old habits and into new, positive directions. Discover more of yourself.

Part of your life's "job description" requires you to take a brain that's gray on the outside and, through all the days of your life, fill it with brightness and color. Suppose your life were suddenly transformed into a box of 64 Crayola crayons. Which colors have had the most use? If you're not fulfilling your dreams, as most people aren't, the black, white, and gray crayons are probably worn down to nubs.

A lifetime commitment to an ever-evolving self is a marriage made in heaven; and heaven-on-earth lies within us as we follow our hearts and pursue our dreams.

"Artists" Are Everywhere

People sometimes look closely at my artwork and say something like, "I'm surprised that you can do this with just pencils and a blank sheet of paper." While a very nice compliment, this implies that artistic expression magically comes from some secret, powerful place. Believe me, it doesn't.

An artist creates by starting with a blank canvas or paper, but never with a blank mind. Human beings cannot create anything without thought. We build upon what we already know. The more we learn and grow, the more fertile our minds become, increasing the likelihood that imaginative ideas will sprout and flourish. Creativity arises from a mix of our life experiences, what our hearts and souls desire, what we study, and the unique reworking of that which already exists.

A new drawing is affected by and made, in part, from all the drawings which preceded it. Each work of art is part of an ongoing education; one more step forward in the incremental process called creation. Nothing new is produced whole and unattached—an artistic island—even though it may appear that way.

Artists aren't wizards; yet, because art is a visual manifestation of creativity, its impact on others can be quite dramatic. Step outside the art arena and you can find the same wonderful creativity expressed in countless other ways. Teachers, scientists, engineers, writers, chefs, surgeons, secretaries, business owners, computer programmers, and many others demonstrate great artistic abilities—perhaps without realizing it.

Steve was a plumber who did work for my parents many years ago. He once showed me photos of an especially challenging plumbing job he had successfully tackled. They pictured a narrow, cramped crawlspace in which he had assembled an innovative line of pipes, running them up into an old house. Obviously his work required great imagination and skill.

Steve was neither a sophisticated nor articulate man, but he was an artist, nonetheless. I remember his pleasure in showing me those crawlspace photographs. He was beaming. Like Handel completing his "Hallelujah Chorus," or Hemingway finishing a short story, Steve, the plumber, felt that same glow of satisfaction experienced by artists working at their creative best.

One autumn day in Rhinebeck, New York, I saw a long line of people waiting outside a small art gallery. They came to see artist Charles Wysocki, wanting him to autograph their copy of his latest book. Seeing that line of eager people stretching down the block, reminded me of my father.

For many years, my parents operated a drive-in restaurant, famous locally for its delicious homemade ice cream, which Dad took great joy in making. A small room within the restaurant housed a huge metal vat. Into it Dad poured the richest dairy cream available, along with a variety of flavors he had spent decades perfecting. The results were incomparably delicious.

A line always formed outside the ice cream room whenever Dad finished a batch of his latest frozen masterpiece. Carhops, cooks, and soda jerks stood clutching cups and spoons, waiting to get a taste of it—fresh from the machine. My father's years of hard work and creative experimentation had combined to produce the best ice cream anywhere. Dad, too, was an artist—the Degás of dairy desserts!

Creativity Is Universal

"I admire your artistic ability," people say to me. "I can't even draw a straight line."

"If that were true," I tell them, "you never would've learned to print your name."

As kids, we sat hunched over sheets of yellow lined paper, gripping thick pencils, slowly, painstakingly printing each letter of the alphabet. We drew lots of straight lines then, along with some beautiful loops and swirls. Later, we graduated to writing and, after much practice, our work on paper often developed a flowing, seamless quality. Don't tell me your handwriting is terrible. That doesn't matter. The point is you can do it.

Handwriting is a skill you acquired and is, quite literally, your own personal, creative "signature." The same people who tell me they can't draw a straight line will purchase my work and often sign their credit card with truly distinctive handwriting. Creativity flows from their fingers, but they don't see it!

Creative potential dwells in all of us. It's a universal trait, waiting to be discovered and embraced. But what do some of us say to ourselves? "Oh, I don't have a creative bone in my body." Unfortunately, this belief becomes our reality, and a vital part of what it means to be human is lost.

We have a critic in our heads who may delight in analyzing our creative thoughts only to find fault with them. Your inner critic is the part of you which says "It can't be done," or "That idea is no good."

Comedian W.C. Fields said, "Critics, to be taken seriously, should be able to create as well as criticize." While your inner critic can't create anything new, it can help you hone, polish, and perfect your work. If it whispers inside your head, "You can't do that," just tell it—in no uncertain terms—to shut up…and then affirm, "I can do it!"

Brainstorming Can Help You Move Ahead

In teaching myself to draw I discovered, quite unexpectedly, an effective way to quiet my inner critic whenever necessary. Sitting with a black and white photograph of comedians Laurel and Hardy and some art paper, I drew a portrait of their faces. The drawing didn't go well. As I endeavored to get a likeness, my inner critic kept up his constant progress report. "Those eyes don't look right…That nose is crooked…The mouth is all wrong….” My eraser got a good workout.

In frustration I finally turned the photograph upside-down and drew it that way. Suddenly, my inner critic quieted down and I was able to freely draw what I saw. Gone were eyes, nose, and mouth. Now I was just copying curves and lines and various shades of gray. I blissfully got lost in my work.

Hours later I turned the paper right-side-up to study the results. While nowhere near perfect, my drawing was obviously a portrait of Laurel and Hardy. I was thrilled! Now my inner critic returned and began giving instructions on how to improve the work. This time his criticism was helpful, guiding me to achieve a better likeness.

I learned a valuable lesson that day. Quieting the inner critic as necessary was essential if I was going to be an artist and create drawings. By turning photographs upside-down, I could work without critiquing every line I put down on paper. I found drawing an eye to be impossible, but drawing the upside-down shape of an eye came easily. My inner critic could be moved aside long enough for me to get a picture onto paper, and then I could invite him back to look at my work and offer good, positive advice.

Each of us has two, separate “people” inside our heads: child/creator and an adult/critic share the same cranium. Each needs to know its proper place. You are their overseer. Your role in the creative process is to engage each of them at the right time, which comes with practice.

Writers know this. They often use brainstorming to silence the adult/critic and allow the child/creator to play. As they come to mind, thoughts on a given topic are written quickly without regard to quality. The point is to fill the page or screen with ideas, to get thoughts down before the critic has a chance to complain about content. Once brainstorming is completed, the critic is welcomed back to organize, edit, and craft the words into a finished work of art.

Better to gather a large volume of information and imaginatively sift through it, than to begin with an inadequate supply of material and seek to find creative gold there. You can whittle away from too large a block of wood in a myriad of ways, but your creative options shrink when you're given only a knife and a Popsicle stick.

In any creative endeavor, you hold the power to keep your adult/critic at arm's length long enough to give your child/creator free rein. The process is a skill, not unlike the scrawling of letters onto yellow paper with a fat pencil. With patience, time, practice, and dynamic desire you can learn to bring forth more of your creative potential without sabotaging it.

Your spontaneous child/creator yells, "Action!" and lets the creative cameras roll. Judgment, your adult/critic, banned from the set during filming, steps in later to edit the footage.

Carry Only the Best for Yourself

To know yourself is your personal challenge. Before you can better appreciate your potential, you need to take a long, hard, honest look at yourself and your desire. The people and events of your life, both past and present, can exert powerful influences on you.

To understand what truly motivates us requires the confrontation of our inner fears and painful memories, which we all have. Too often, though, we allow them to shape our entire approach to living. But, being aware of them, as we move forward, learn, and grow, can help us put everything into a better perspective.

Recognizing how past criticisms, injustices, and failures influence the way you act—and react—today, is essential for you to break free from old, limiting thoughts. To know yourself is to uncover the truth that you are stronger than your fear. No matter what fears you may have, you are in control. You can take action to overcome them.

You've been walking around inside your own skin your whole life. Tell me, who's in a better position than you to know your personal doubts, fears, and insecurities? Who, but you, has the deepest insight to your dreams and desires? Who is closest to your potential talents and abilities?

Teachers, clergy, counselors, leaders, mentors, and perhaps others can guide you to better understand yourself and your motives, but the decision to act in your own best interest always rests with you. Ultimately, you're in control of how you choose to relate to yourself and the world. When you stop to think about it, that's a tremendous amount of power. Stop to think about it…then act on it!

Picture your personal challenges as fitting neatly into a container the size of your head. During your lifetime so far, you've managed to haul that container and all of its garbage around, but feel free to dump the unwanted contents any time you choose. Carry only the best for yourself. Deep down inside you probably know what you need to do.

Clichés Can Be Uplifting

Why write a book about the elements of success? Most people have heard them expressed in phrases such as, "Believe in yourself!" "Follow your dream!" "Be disciplined!" "Never give up!" "Do whatever it takes!" and "Make it happen!" These were clichés long before we walked the planet. We've heard them umpteen times. But have we embraced them, ingested them, and then made them a core part of who we are?

Some of us take clichés and personalize them in the form of negative self-talk—giving ourselves various excuses for not achieving our dreams. We choose to stay where we are by the negative cliché thoughts we hold about ourselves and our circumstances. The excuses we cling to become the steel bars we fashion into a personal prison, a safe…but sorry…little world called "but."

- "I would believe in myself, but…"
- "I'd like to follow my dream, but…"
- "I could be disciplined, but…"
- "I wouldn't have given up, but…"
- "I would have done whatever it takes, but…"
- "I would have made it happen, but…"

Such "but" distortions of perfectly fine clichés may be like warm blankets, tucked all around to keep us safe from those monsters—change, risk, and vulnerability—that lurk under the bed.

We may look at our situations and find so many so-called reasons why our life circumstances preclude the fulfillment of our dreams. If so, this becomes our reality.

People visiting my booth at arts festivals sometimes say, "Oh! I have your art." I thank them, but when I ask, "Which pictures do you own?" often they cannot recall the scenes they've bought. Even when my work has been decorating their walls for years, some customers find themselves struggling to remember which framed prints they've purchased.

I laugh when this happens and tell them not to feel bad. I experience the same problem, and I don't think it's because my work is less memorable than that of other artists. Day after day, we see the same pictures until they no longer register on our minds. There the art hangs, in plain view, yet we seem to look right through it.

"I like to rotate my pictures," I tell people. "When we change the scenery on our walls, it helps to keep our vision fresh." What's true for artwork also holds true for clichés. For example, we're all familiar with the following lines:

- "Never put off until tomorrow what you can do today."
- "Haste makes waste."
- "You can lead a horse to water, but you can't make him drink."
- "A fool and his money are soon parted."

- "You reap what you sow."

Through the years, we've heard these and other similar clichés so often that they may no longer have much impact on us. That's unfortunate. The reason clichés are so durable is because they usually state truths. The best advice is often the oldest, most basic information we know.

Don't take clichés for granted simply because they've been hanging on your mind's wall for a long time. Take time to really see them, hear them, and understand what practical applications they can have in your own life. Use them to your advantage.

Why Would You Want to Act Like a Bird?

When a bird sees its reflection in a windowpane, it often reacts as if the image is another bird about to invade its territory. Its response is then to fly into the glass to attack the "intruder". If the impact causes no injury, the bird may repeat its attack, crashing against the window again and again, to get at that "enemy" bird, until it finally renders itself stunned, injured, or dead. The bird doesn't realize that its injuries are self-inflicted.

We watch this happen and sadly shake our heads. "Poor bird," we may say. Yet, people often engage in similar, self-destructive behavior. We may continually fly into the glass of negative thought patterns which have hurt us in the past. We may crash against the same harmful circumstances many times over, all the while failing to see how we're contributing to our own pain and unhappiness.

Some people are worse to themselves than our feathered friends. Some of us understand the harm we're doing to ourselves, but we keep doing it anyway! For example, a bird may say:

- "I've always flown into the glass."
- "I know this is hurting me, but what else can I do?"

- "I deserve to fly into windowpanes."
- "If I fly hard and fast enough, I'll break through this glass."
- "You can blame me for crashing against the window, but I didn't put it there."

Maybe it's high time for some of us to change our flight patterns!

In performing from the sheet music of our daily lives, we may often repeat the same tune with little variation, no longer hearing the notes we're playing. We think and act in established habitual ways because they're familiar to us. Though they may bring unhappiness and be detrimental to our personal growth, they're still what we know best. The creature of habit may be slowly curling itself around our creative potential, eventually strangling it.

You may want to think of habit and routine as comfortable old clothes. Though they're frayed and out of style, you continue to wear them. But they do limit the places where you can go. Get rid of them so you can move on.

Get Rid of the Trash

Twice a year, our small town has a special trash and clean-up day. Unwanted large appliances and bulky items, which ordinarily couldn't be put out with the weekly garbage, are picked up and taken away.

Wouldn't it be wonderful if people used the same approach to rid their minds of lazy, useless, negative thoughts? Dusty old prejudices; worn out, habitual ways of doing things; and dog-eared opinions need to be dragged outside and deposited at the curb.

I enjoy listening to radio personality, Dr. Laura Schlessinger. "Dr. Laura," as she calls herself, is a controversial woman, largely because she holds people accountable for their actions. Her radio program is designed to promote moral behavior. This ethical stance was bound to make her unpopular with some listeners. Playwright Henrik Ibsen said, "Never put on your good trousers to go out fighting for truth and justice."

A scientist by training, Dr. Laura says habits could be more than just familiar patterns of behavior. They may actually become hard-wired into us, by establishing neural pathways in the brain, reinforced every time we engage in specific thoughts or actions.

She believes in "manual override," the power of the human will to overcome unwanted patterns set down in our brains. Dr. Laura used this technique to manage, and ultimately eliminate, her own crippling panic attacks.

"This act of will may be excruciatingly difficult," she says, "but it isn't impossible." Meeting tough challenges in this way, and conquering them, can change your life dramatically. In the face of some difficult task, our *lack* of will can create a glare so bright that we want to hide in the shadows of 'impossibility.'"

Rule as a monarch over your kingdom of thought. Sadly, some choose to abdicate their power to other people. If you are one of them, reclaim your power—it belongs to you!

Keep Your Mental Battery Charged!

Every human being comes equipped with a remarkable, permanent mental battery. Failures and setbacks may drain it of a lot of power, but it generally has some energy left. Fortunately, our internal battery is fully rechargeable, provided we attach it to currents of positive thoughts that are used to provide the energy necessary to take action.

It's the supply of optimism that keeps our battery recharging during the tough times. We experience it as a spirited determination to be flexible and adapt as setbacks occur, a willingness to see opportunity in any failure, and a desire to find whatever resources are needed to move again toward our goals and dreams.

By contrast, any mental battery attached to a negative drain is further weakened during periods of crisis. Drains of cynicism and hopelessness deplete its current, which is experienced as withdrawal in the face of obstacles, a refusal to overcome challenges, and a feeling of being victimized rather than empowered, especially in moments of crisis.

Attempting to avoid facing problems, some in this deteriorating state engage in self-destructive behavior. Left unchecked, this continual drain results in a dead battery. Unless they get a charge of optimism... and get moving again while constantly recharging their battery... they'll find themselves getting lower and lower on current, potentially going "dead." At their present level of thinking...their low state of charge...they don't have the energy to overcome their problems and move forward.

So be sure to plug yourself into a powerful positive source now, so you can rejuvenate the energy necessary to sustain you when challenges arise. Keep your mental battery fully charged, ready for anything.

The most powerful, mind-altering "drug" available to you is a positive change of attitude, which produces a continual feeling of gratitude, the foundation for a happy life. Simply taking a moment to mentally run through what you are grateful for can give you a positive charge.

Your mind possesses incredible power. You picture things mentally daily. Your imagination continually projects thoughts of what you want and expect from life onto your mental movie screen. You can picture anything you desire, so go ahead and create your life as a stirring epic!

Positive Statements Can Help You Overcome and Achieve

It's been said that nothing that happens to you in life is bad, provided you learn and grow from the experience.

Challenges and upheavals are inevitable in everyone's life. "This, too, shall pass," as Abraham Lincoln said, is a great adage to keep in mind. If we don't do something about it, the stress associated with a traumatic experience can stay with us for a long time, affecting our ability to conquer adversity.

Stress is a part of life. We all need to deal with it. Fortunately, we can control our response to it. Rather than denying the stress—make it work for you. Harness yourself with the right mental attitude.

The Chinese word for crisis consists of two brush strokes. One stroke signifies danger; the other, opportunity. Why not make this part of your personal credo?

A crisis is an opportunity!

Have you ever reached a new level in a relationship because of how well you handled the crisis that person presented to you? It simply turned out to be an opportunity to strengthen the relationship.

Viewing problems, challenges, and situations as golden opportunities to learn and grow can enhance your health. Scientific research has demonstrated this. Think of your mind as a chemist and your brain as the laboratory. As you think optimistic thoughts, it causes reactions in your brain—releasing chemicals that positively affect your central nervous system, organ function, and immune system's ability to resist disease.

When you focus on positive possibilities in times of setback, your chemist-mind also becomes your personal physician! Crises will actually strengthen you and improve your health—when you choose to *learn and grow*, not just go, through them positively and confidently.

Our minds work for us or against us. Have faith that everything will work out if you're faced with the possibility of failure. Consciously adjust your mental attitude to find solutions. As a result, you'll grow stronger and more confident through challenges.

The late Dr. Norman Vincent Peale spent decades instructing people to fill their minds with meaningful, positive statements. Here are just a few for your mental files:

- "I can if I think I can."
- "Faith can solve any personal problem."
- "I was made to handle challenges."

These aren't just simple, pleasant mantras to make you feel good for the moment. Take them to heart and use them to actively establish a positive mental foundation for yourself. As challenges arise, you will stay strong as you work your way through them. When problems and setbacks rattle your life like seismic waves, you won't collapse. You'll remain structurally sound.

As you repeat these positive statements to yourself, feel them working to strengthen you. Remember, you were born with the potential to succeed in every area of your life. Have the faith and reassurance that you're not alone as you deal with challenges, and persist until you handle them successfully.

As you build internal fortitude, challenges stimulate and activate your creative capabilities. You respond to them with an enthusiastic, determined spirit, while overcoming and advancing. Stressful situations inspire you into productive action when you choose to look at them as opportunities.

Saying, "I can't" cuts you off from the possibilities. You would be allowing fear to immobilize you. Why do that to yourself? Fortunately, thoughts aren't chiseled into your mind; they're only written in mental chalk. With your will to think positively you can overcome negative patterns. As you practice daily, you can erase and replace them.

You were made to learn, grow, and move forward. Your faith, courage, and resourcefulness will help you plot the best course to follow. Your brain was given to you as standard equipment. Faith, courage, and dedication to overcome obstacles are options you need to buy. Your character is the currency. Nothing you do can be out of character for you. What you do demonstrates it. Build yours through a positive response to life's challenges. Be an excellent example for others to follow. Everyone can benefit.

Dr. Peale's positive thinking contributed to nearly a century of robust living, learning, and leading. His life was a great testimonial to the effectiveness of positive statements.

Choose Your Words Carefully

Intimidation. Who hasn't been gripped by fear in some moment of crisis? We've all felt threatened at times. We may feel intimidated by any unwelcomed change of circumstances. We may respond to divorce, a career or business setback, or a sudden health challenge in such a way as to undermine our confidence and make ourselves afraid.

Let's take a closer look at that word, *intimidation*. Play with it. Remove the letters *id* from the middle of it and set them aside for a moment. Now, what word remains? *Intimation.* To intimate is to suggest or make known indirectly; to hint at something. A challenge or failure, or any crisis in life, is also an intimation to us...when we search for the opportunities hidden there.

Now retrieve the letters *id* and capitalize them: *I.D.* That, of course, is the abbreviation for *identification*. What is your identity in times of crisis? Are you threatened and fearful, or are you, instead, a bold seeker of the positive possibilities inherent in any ordeal?

Intimidation and intimation are two powerful words. Which one is used most often in your mental vocabulary? One denies, the other affirms, your innate creative resources. *Choose your words carefully!*

Whenever doubt or fear calls on you, simply let your internal voicemail take it, and reply with this message: "Sorry, I'm working toward fulfilling my potential right now. Take my number off your call list—and don't *ever* call me again!"

Choose Optimism for Mental Health

For every positive a cynic cites a negative. But for every negative an optimist cites a positive. Both are correct, but only one enjoys a healthy mind and a happy, productive life. Anyone who dwells on life's unpleasant aspects is a starving person seated in a fine restaurant for a free meal, angry for being served bread that wasn't warm.

I once knew a knowledgeable man I'll call Don. His mind retained virtually everything he read, and the broad range of his education was impressive. But all that knowledge hadn't brought him much wisdom. Why? Don was a cynic. Positive thoughts stopped in for a visit but quickly left; whereas negative thoughts took a permanent room upstairs.

Since his inner world was a mess, he only found fault with the world around him. He avoided the fear and discomfort associated with personal growth by withdrawing into himself, complaining about all that was wrong with the world…everyone and everything in it…and could cite plenty of examples!

But how does someone show such a lack of love for him- or herself and others, ignoring the value and beauty of what many of us consider the finer things of life: flower gardens, scenic views, libraries, art museums, theaters, concert halls, and such?

A callous spirit grows to suffocate appreciation and gratitude—the very keys to happiness. You cannot effectively act as both Nature's work of art and Her art critic. Either live and breathe Her creativity or tear yourself apart. Which course of action will you choose?

Don preferred the security of a known ditch to the adventure of an unknown road. "I can't change who I am," he argued. By saying that, Don reduced himself, intellectually, to the lowest level. "I can't change" makes about as much sense as "I can't blink." It really means "I *won't* change."

The potential to change is built into us, like eyelids that open and close automatically, and can also be done so at will as well. Just make a decision and a more determined effort to accomplish the change. If we won't change, we've denied our potential.

Frankly, to be around Don for any length of time was both frustrating and emotionally draining. His attitude about himself, and life, was self-crippling. But he refused to seek help. Don saw himself as a failure, and he was one—by choice. "Cynic" is just another name for someone who has given up. However, if a seed of desire, no matter how small, still exists within us, it can be nurtured and grown.

Healthy-thinking people patiently lay one brick of positive action upon another to create a larger, stronger self. Distance yourself from negative people who would pick away at your mortar rather than encourage you or help you lay more positive bricks.

Know that a certain percentage of people will always disagree with you, regardless of what action you take. Some of them may enviously laugh and jeer at you from the sidelines—precisely because they're on the sidelines! If others criticize your efforts, they always say more about themselves than they do about you. It's just a reflection of their unhappy thinking. If they were happy themselves, they would look for the good and applaud you.

Egotism Has No Place in Our Lives

A few years ago, I visited a large art show where the work of a fine watercolorist caught my attention. The details in his paintings were so exquisite that I felt moved to tell him so.

"It's wonderful to see the depth of realism you capture with your watercolors," I said. "Being a colored pencil artist myself, I can appreciate the talent and time involved in creating such detailed work. Your paintings are beautiful."

He looked down his nose at me and said sarcastically, "Well, you have to learn to draw before you can paint." He then turned away.

I stood there feeling stung, dazed. "What's with this guy?" I wondered. "Here I've just paid him an honest, sincere compliment, and he insults me!" I left his booth thinking, "Wow! What an unhappy man. How sad..."

People at peace with themselves don't feel compelled to belittle anyone. A sturdy fabric of self-confidence is never woven from threads of inferiority put on others. That talented, but pompous, watercolorist who dismissed me with a verbal slap needs help and loving kindness, but he'd probably refuse it. Egotism often masks insecurity.

Puffing up your ego in an effort to feel better about yourself is somewhat like upgrading a wardrobe to improve the health of a deceased person just before the viewing. It's all show. There's no substance to it.

Talented people who find joy in their work seldom display egos. They quietly go about their business, content to be conduits for creativity. They're humbled by the realization that creativity flows through them from some mysterious, marvelous source.

Never allow yourself to be rattled by egotistical people who put down you or your efforts. Be above retaliation. Don't waste your valuable energy on them. Just wish them well and go on your way.

Eleanor Roosevelt kept this sign hanging in her Hyde Park, New York, home: "No one can make you feel inferior without your permission." Remember that whenever someone tries to diminish you. Take a comical view of such people. Arrogant egos stand all wobbly in the scheme of things, like a boastful drunk pulled to the side of the road and asked to walk a straight line.

Let Go of Regrets

We can stare at an old photograph all day but doing so can never change its composition. We attempt to do just that if we've ever dwelled on the past with regret.

Through the years, I've met so many people tortured by regrets. They dissect the past as if it were their lab assignment. Even worse, they've barricaded themselves in the stale lab and refuse to come out to enjoy the fresh air of the present.

Two of the most powerful words in the English language are "let go." If you've made foolish choices and embarrassing mistakes in the past, congratulations! You've joined the ranks of everyone who has ever lived. However, if you've learned from your errors, made any needed adjustments, and left all your regrets behind, you are among the minority. Once again, congratulations!

It's impossible to close the book on your past if you focus on, memorize, and repeat everything written there. Commit yourself now to letting go. If you need to make some apologies, do so. No one can travel back to yesterday, so why keep planning an itinerary for the trip?

Take Personal Responsibility

You can believe in your potential for growth, or you can tear yourself down with the words, "I can't." In life, we choose to be either architects or demolition experts. You are in control of which one you are. You can either wield the wrecking ball or build a meaningful life. It's up to you.

A while back, I watched a documentary concerning the Revolutionary War and birth of America. What impressed me most about our Founding Fathers was the great faith they held in our ability, as individuals, to govern ourselves.

When Thomas Jefferson wrote the Declaration of Independence, his expectations of the American people were high. He believed freedom required individuals to assume responsibility for their own lives, while dedicating themselves to the pursuit of excellence as a means of keeping the nation strong.

Were Jefferson to visit America today, he'd be appalled by the growing number of people who no longer hold themselves accountable for their lives and behaviors. Ours has, unfortunately, become a society teeming with so-called victims, many of whom use their challenges as excuses for why they "can't" live the life they think they're entitled to.

Sure, we've been challenged by dysfunctional parents, abusive spouses, alcoholism, drug abuse and other addictions, corporate downsizing, the tobacco industry, violence, negative news, and even poverty. We talk about the disadvantaged as if their condition were a congenital trait, like blue eyes or freckles.

We all have our challenges—big and small. Winners use their challenges to strengthen themselves; in overcoming them they springboard themselves to success.

The world doesn't owe anyone a living...it was here first, and Father Time waits for no one. Many whine and complain, pointing fingers of blame at others for what are really their own personal failures and an unwillingness to change themselves for the better. Choosing to play victim is just another way of saying, "The dog ate my homework." It's disempowering, losing behavior.

Refusing to hold yourself accountable for your failures is like standing in front of a mirror, denying your own reflection. "But people do experience hard times and setbacks," critics argue. "Shouldn't we offer them compassionate support?"

Of course! But what's the best, most empowering way to do so? It all depends. "Sink or swim" is a metaphorical-type of advice often given by those who would use the power of tough love. But you could also encourage someone by saying, "If I can do it, then you can too. Here's how."

Regardless of the approach, no amount of commiseration or compassion alone will help anyone. The most compassionate thing you can do for someone is to empower them by saying something like, "I believe in you, and I'll even show you the way. You can do it!" You're giving them a hand up, not a hand out.

People will usually live up to—or down to—your expectations of them. "I believe in you" is no simplistic comment. It's a statement of faith and great compassion. To help people realize the vast power they possess to change themselves and their circumstances is an act of true kindness. To hold people accountable for their own behaviors is to give them respect and dignity. To expect the best from people is to show them love. You can teach people to swim, but you can't swim for them.

A Dangerous Super-Glue

The strongest glue in the world doesn't come in a tube or plastic bottle. The powerful ingredients consist of four simple words: "It's Not My Fault!" Using these words together is the surest way to keep yourself stuck wherever you are in life. They're guaranteed to immobilize you right there, on the spot.

Roberta was eight when she began playing the violin. Her passionate desire for it was so strong that she practiced hours on end. As she developed her dynamic desire, it brought forth a genuine talent.

At 12, she was taking private lessons with a distinguished professor of music, whose guidance helped her enhance her knowledge and musical ability. By her senior year in high school, Roberta had won first chair in an All-State Orchestra, defeating many talented students for this coveted position.

She received scholarship offers from several colleges. During an audition for enrollment at one prestigious music school, the judges were suspicious that Roberta had broken the rules when she sight-read an unfamiliar composition perfectly. Her performance was so excellent that the judges thought someone had sneaked the music to her prior to the audition! The stunning results of her second test, using different music, left the judges feeling apologetic... and astounded.

"That was my peak accomplishment," Roberta recalled at age 40. "Afterward, everything began to fall apart."

"My mother didn't want any of her kids to leave home," she shared. "Mom wouldn't accept that things change and that life moves on. Looking back, I can now see how unhappy and manipulative she was. Her tears had a powerful effect on me. I felt guilty for wanting to go away to college."

"What about your father?" I asked her.

"Dad was working three jobs and couldn't be bothered. He found it easier just to agree with Mom."

Despite the scholarship offers, Roberta chose to enroll in a smaller music school within her state. She was just miserable. "I resented my parents," she lamented, "actually blaming them for *my* decision not to attend one of the best-ranked music schools in the country—on a full scholarship, no less!"

When Roberta told her parents she needed a better violin for scholastic competitions, they said the money wasn't available.

"Why didn't you take a part-time job and buy the violin yourself?" I asked her.

"It was easier to make excuses. Professionals need to play eight hours daily if they want to compete successfully. But I told myself it was my parents' fault that I wasn't practicing enough, because they wouldn't give me the proper instrument."

The university Roberta attended was known as a "party school," and unfortunately she joined the party with enthusiasm. Late night reveling and binge drinking soon hastened her academic decline.

"When professors criticized my performance, I accused them of being unreasonable and intolerant. What a great excuse-maker I was in those days," she says, shaking her head sadly. "I blamed my parents and uncaring professors—everyone but myself. I held that nothing was my fault."

Roberta quit college after her freshman year, moving into a modest apartment off-campus and taking a food server job to support herself. But her partying and drinking continued. "Alcohol gave me instant ease and comfort," she remembers. "It deadened the pain."

She also sought escape from herself in a string of relationships with men who had losing attitudes and behaviors. "I made terrible choices in men," she says. "Of course, I didn't see things that way at the time." She just blamed men.

For Roberta, her "It's Not My Fault!" super-glue kept her stuck in a world where she believed family, professors, and the men she dated all conspired to victimize her. "Everyone took advantage of me," she says, "and I felt oh so sorry for myself!" She had hit bottom.

Roberta sought treatment for alcoholism and began her long road to psychological recovery. "To face my life honestly wasn't easy," she admits. "Old ways of thinking are comfortable—even when they're destroying you." But she stopped using the super-glue of blame.

Sober for 20 years, Roberta is now a happily married mother of two, whose home-based sales business is thriving. (She also enjoys plays violin in a community orchestra.) "I learned the hard way that my thoughts create everything in my life," she says. "*I'm* the one responsible for the kind of life I live."

Accountability is the only effective solvent for detaching yourself from the super-glue of blame. Bitterness, resentment, and envy also dissolve when the decision is made to accept full responsibility for the who, what, where, and why of your life.

"Responsibility educates," wrote 19th Century reformer Wendell Phillips. The decision to assume responsibility for all your failures, as well as your successes, is your most vital tool for rapid learning and personal growth. It greatly strengthens your capacity to live a rich, rewarding life.

Take Charge—*Get Out from Under the Circumstances!*

"If only my situation were different, I could do what I want." Sound familiar? Perhaps you've said this to yourself. If your brain were a clock radio, this statement would be the snooze button.

Wake up!

Thinking, action-oriented people don't shrug their shoulders and accept their lot in life. They demand a lot from life and themselves—and they work to get it.

"If only my situation were different" is as though your present circumstances were flypaper, and you were the fly. Your life, as it exists today, is a partially completed book. You grip the pen or keyboard and, if you're not happy with what you've been writing, start a new chapter.

Remember when, as a kid in school, you committed some minor infraction and the teacher made you write something like, "I will not talk in class," one hundred times? Along with writer's cramp, you also experienced the joy of taking the paper home for your parents to sign.

Well, here we sit today with our life's book, and what one sentence do many of us repeatedly write? "If only my situation were different, I could do what I want."

Page after page may be filled with this mantra of complete resignation. If we insist on putting down the same thoughtless, negative, disempowering sentence, at least let's be honest. In this case, our statement would read: "In my present situation I'm not going to do anything to achieve what I want."

Some people say they want to soar, but it can't be done without spreading the wings of self-belief. Get out from under the circumstances and make something good happen.

Responsibility is like a boomerang. If you throw it hard at others, or at past or present circumstances, be prepared to duck. It will surely come back and hit you if you don't move out of the way.

Take complete responsibility for your life. Know that you can never again honestly blame your failures or unhappiness on anyone, or anything, but yourself. Realize that all of the choices you've made have led you precisely to the place you now occupy.

Your choices—not circumstances—have created what and where you are today. Those who claim to be the victims of circumstance assume the impossible—that they've lost their innate power to choose. That's just not true. You *can*, indeed, choose, no matter what life throws your way.

Playwright George Bernard Shaw said, "People are always blaming their circumstances for what they are in life. I don't believe in circumstances. The people who get on in this world are the people who get up and look for the circumstances they want and, if they can't find them, make them."

"But circumstances are often out of our control," one man said to me recently. "They can dictate our lives," he argued. "We don't always have choices."

Granted, some people are in more challenging situations than others. Some have higher hurdles to clear. But it's how we choose to deal with them that determines our ultimate success or failure. The truth is that the most successful people usually come from the ranks of the most challenged.

In the ballpark of any circumstance, the right attitude will always hit the ball—and maybe even a home run.

One of my favorite people is Abraham Lincoln. We hear his name today and he may not seem real to us. He's a legend, seemingly larger than life. But Lincoln was human. Throughout his life, he suffered periods of depression so severe he'd remain in bed for days at a time. As president, he was not well liked. Editorial cartoonists of the day often portrayed him as a baboon.

Lincoln watched helplessly as first one son—and later another—died in childhood from disease. His wife, Mary, was a mentally unstable woman, known to embarrass and humiliate him in public. Lincoln presided over a nation being torn in two by the Civil War. He saw more than 600,000 of his fellow Americans die in that conflict. But Lincoln understood that it's our responses to the challenges of life that either elevate or destroy us. "Most folks," he said, "are about as happy as they make up their minds to be."

Lincoln stands as a shining example of how to take responsibility in life. He chose to endure. Take responsibility for your life and the potential within you to overcome any obstacle to success. The only limits on you, ultimately, are those you place upon yourself by not believing in yourself. Remember, you *always* have choices.

To dwell on what you would do "if circumstances were different" is to sit out in the rain, surrounded by closed umbrellas, and just daydream about how much better you'd feel if you were dry.

"If circumstances were different" is a sensible lament only if you find yourself bound and gagged with a bomb in your lap—and that bomb has just stopped ticking.

"I have no choice" is just another choice.

Don't Stand Too Close

Imagine yourself in an art museum. Your face is positioned two inches away from a fine painting as you stare at what appears to be a glob of some color brushed hastily onto the canvas. "This Rembrandt doesn't do much for me," you may think to yourself. "I don't see what all the fuss is about."

Take a few steps back and, suddenly, that brushstroke begins to make some sense to you. Put a little more distance between you and the painting, and that glob of color melds perfectly with the others to create a beautiful work of art.

As observers of life, all of us are probably guilty, to some degree, of standing too close. We sometimes take life out of context. Caught up in our daily routines and responsibilities, preoccupied with our challenges, we may fail to step back and see ourselves for what we really are: part of the masterpiece of the world—a living, breathing work of art.

Your life and the planet on which you live hold little meaning when separated from their broader context. Stand back each day to see yourself as the marvelous brushstroke you are. Step back farther and understand that you also hold your own palette, brushes, and an infinite combination of colors for your use. In reality, you are both paint and painter, here to make your own work of art within this art gallery called the world.

Playwright Neil Simon said that his sense of humor was due, in part, to an ability to step back and observe himself during moments of personal challenge. This detachment, in the middle of emotional times, has enabled him to see virtually any situation from a comical perspective.

To change ingrained patterns of negative thought and action, we need to engage in this kind of objective observation. Unproductive attitudes and behaviors, many of which we've been hauling around with us for years, are best dealt with from a fresh and distant point of view.

When you practice becoming the mental eyewitness to your moments of fear and negativity, questioning the "why" of any insecure feelings you may have, you'll begin to see the role that unthinking habit has played in sabotaging your potential for growth. A more objective and amused recognition of your personal weaknesses gives you new insight into those old patterns of thought, enabling you to more easily break away from the hold they once had on you.

It's only when we fully understand the reasons for our self-limiting attitudes and non-productive behaviors that we're able to change in positive, lasting ways.

Look Outside Yourself

We all have so much untapped potential. Accept yourself, while recognizing that any elements of weakness or inferiority you feel can be offset by focusing on your inner strengths. Yes, we all have them!

Don't deny any insecure facets of your personality that you may have. Acknowledge them. For the moment, they're still part of you, but they're certainly not all that you are. To be limited by feelings of deficiency is to ignore the potential for greatness that's also a part of you. Utilizing more of it can bring you greater inner peace and fulfillment.

Why is it so easy for many of us to view our flaws honestly, yet have such difficulty seeing the potential excellence inside? All of us also need to take a truthful approach to what's positive about ourselves. There are elements in each of us that we can build upon to achieve success.

To excel, focus on and develop your inner strengths and then give of yourself to others, directing your positive qualities into a cause larger than yourself. By looking outward, not inward, we soon forget any insecurity we may have and begin to know the joy of contributing our unique, dynamic desire developed talents as we focus on helping others.

As a young man, Abraham Lincoln was a self-absorbed neurotic. At 32 he said, "I am now the most miserable man living. If what I feel were equally distributed to the whole human family, there would not be one cheerful face on earth."

It's hard to believe this is the same man who grew to become one of the greatest presidents the US has ever known. You can more easily understand Lincoln's transformation from a self-absorbed introvert to skillful leader when you see the greater causes to which he eventually dedicated his life. By focusing outward, Lincoln brought forth the best from within himself, and you can too. Like he did, dedicate your life to a good cause.

Develop a Sense of Humor

One personality trait essential to our sanity is a healthy sense of humor. Lincoln certainly had that. His self-deprecating humor and a willingness to accept his own deficiencies were part of his greatness. A woman once accused him of being two-faced. "Madam," he said, "if I had two faces, do you think I would choose this one?"

Humor is our internal mechanic, and it's there for us to improve our relationship with. It inspects, adjusts, and lubricates our mental machinery to keep it in good working order.

When we maintain a spirit of playfulness, it keeps alive that child-like sense of awe and wonder about life and our own potential as human beings. Humor cultivates our imagination and nurtures our creative spontaneity. Coupled with dynamic desire, these are invaluable tools in the pursuit of our dreams.

Humor relieves tension by removing us from ourselves and making us—like Neil Simon—detached observers. From this perspective, we can usually think more clearly about problems. The detachment humor provides gives us a pair of fresh eyes.

Humor reins in our ego and feelings of self-importance. It helps us maintain a healthy attitude about life and our place in the world. If you can't laugh at yourself, you're missing out on some of the funniest comedy material available.

A sure sign of self-acceptance is the ability to laugh at yourself. To do that, you need to let go of your ego, step outside of yourself, and take a more objective look at who you really are. That requires a degree of maturity that most need to develop.

Finally, humor touches emotions that are felt universally. Victor Borge liked to say, "The shortest distance between two people is a good laugh." Through humor we recognize our common fears and insecurities. Good comedy makes for camaraderie and light-heartedness.

It's important to live larger than yourself, to dedicate your desires toward serving others. Focus on others. It's essential to becoming truly successful. You'll also find it much more fun than just being self-absorbed. As you serve others, you'll get to observe the world from their unique perspectives. You'll learn about so many new things—it'll make your life much more interesting.

You may consider yourself a little shy. Many people are, even if they appear not to be. By nature, I'm a shy person. That shyness is a personality deficiency I recognize, and I'm working on it. Part of the process is writing this book. I refuse to allow my self-absorption, which causes my shyness, to detract from the potential good I can do.

Some time ago, I discovered this story by Margaret Lee Runbeck in a yellowed, 1947 edition of *Reader's Digest*. She recalled being a shy, awkward young woman of 18, sitting on the auditorium stage at her high school graduation. Because of her scholastic achievement, Margaret was assigned the task of delivering the valedictory address. She was a nervous wreck.

On stage with her that day was the commencement speaker, in whom she confided, "I'm scared to death." He smiled kindly, and this is what he said:

"I'll tell you a secret, and then you'll never need to be scared again. Everyone on earth is shy, self-conscious, and unsure of himself. Everybody's timid about meeting strangers. So if you'll just spend the first minute you're in the presence of a stranger trying to help him feel comfortable, you'll never suffer from self-consciousness again."

Margaret Lee Runbeck always remembered that friendly stranger's advice. She applied it that day and throughout her life. Margaret often wished she could have recalled his name, to thank him for his kindness. Many years later, while cleaning out her attic, she came across her old, high school Commencement Day program. On the front cover it said, "Commencement Address, by Assistant Secretary of the Navy, the Honorable Franklin D. Roosevelt."

" *Our destiny changes with our thought; we shall become what we wish to become, do what we wish to do, when our habitual thought corresponds with our desire.* "

—Orison Swett Marden

Chapter 2
What's Your Purpose or Calling?

True happiness and joy is in the pursuit of your dream—your purpose or calling—when you choose the path that's right for you.

Ask people what they want and they may say, "I want to be happy" or "I want to be rich." Although these desires are understandable, they're not just going to fall out of the sky and drop into their lap.

Desiring these things without doing what needs to be done that can make them a reality may leave them forever frustrated, as directly seeking them does not lead to a happy, prosperous life. They are byproducts of earnestly pursuing your purpose or calling and can come only through making that journey, fully participating in the process. Don't confuse them with goals in and of themselves.

Take a direct aim at happiness, and you'll instantly lose sight of the target you need to aim for in order to live a happy, joyful life. But do what's right for you regarding your purpose or calling, and happiness and joy, as well as monetary rewards, can be yours along the way.

Dr. Benjamin Spock, the baby doctor, expressed it well when he said, "Happiness is mostly a by-product of doing what makes us feel fulfilled." I also like Bette Davis's thoughts on the subject. "To fulfill a dream," she said, "to be allowed to sweat over lonely labor, to be given the chance to create, is the meat and potatoes of life. The money is the gravy."

While happiness and money can be found in the process of doing, the search for happiness in money or material possessions themselves can be, at best, fleeting. It's like a dying man's last wish for a new mattress.

It's foolish to look for personal fulfillment in things. "If I could just have that new car, house, relationship, or job, I'd be happy." Wrong. You may have momentary happiness. But when the novelty wears off, you'll be looking for happiness in something else—which can be a virtually endless cycle.

Look at people who achieve sudden fame. The money pours in, and they can buy anything they want. I could fill the rest of this book with names of men and women who seemingly "have it all" yet still feel empty inside and miserable. Along with all the new possessions came their same, old, flawed ways of thinking. They were always looking outside themselves for happiness.

Such people are decorating a house with no foundation. They can paint it, landscape it, and fill it with the finest furniture—only to see it collapse. No amount of possessions can furnish the empty space within.

An English professor I knew in college, Dr. Philip Flynn, described this challenge as "the little voice." It tells us we could be happy if only we had that new _____. So we may be spending our lives chasing after things, expecting possessions to bring us fulfillment. But that restless, little voice always returns to tell us we need even *more* things. The race often ends only when we do.

Here's a short verse I wrote to describe the situation:

A change in looks
Or what you own
Or work you choose to do,
A move from here to somewhere else
And still you live with you.
The only change that really counts
When all is done or said,
Is ever hid from public view
And happens in your head.

Those who believe they need a change of scenery need to first look to their inner landscapes. Searching for external answers to internal challenges is like playing the piano with a guitar pick. As the cartoon character Ziggy says, "Wherever I go, there I am!"

Nothing can bring happiness or joy to us. We are the vessel in which it is contained. Take any desire you may have to acquire more money, material possessions, leisure, or something else and direct that hunger toward the accumulation of more knowledge about yourself.

Increase ownership of your inner strength and potential, grow your store of talents and abilities, gain increased wisdom, and develop more compassion for others, and you'll become one of the richest people in the world. While money does matter, your courage, character, consistency, compassion, and creativity always matter more.

Recognize Your Passion and Develop Dynamic Desire for It

What are *you* passionate about? The answer is different for everyone reading this book. Each of us is born with and also discovers passions and desires as we move forward pursuing and developing them. In so doing, our joy, happiness, and an enriched life experience comes.

Remember, we're all gifted with desire—the dynamic development of which leads to our contributions to the world. Are you using your gifts or just playing with the packaging materials?

Given the choice, what would you love to be doing? Stop and take some time to answer that. Then, when you believe in yourself and take total responsibility for creating the outcomes you want in life, you'll know that you have the choice to work toward doing what you love. It's up to you.

"Success," according to Malcolm Forbes, "follows doing what you want to do. There is no other way to be successful."

What you're passionate about is what you'll be happiest about working toward accomplishing. As you develop dynamic desire, it'll see you through any frustrations and setbacks you face while striving to reach your goal or dream. It's an ingredient essential to all success. Life without dynamic desire is dull and boring.

"I don't want people who want to dance," said choreographer George Ballanchine, "I want people who *have to* dance."

Frank Sinatra once listened to his son deliver a half-hearted singing performance and yelled at him, "You're contributing nothing if you aren't excited by what you're doing." Whatever you love to do, whatever subject excites you, whatever that gift is, pour yourself into it! Give it your all. Do what is in your heart of hearts to do.

The rewards for labor are to be found in the labor itself. Leisure gives you the momentary pleasure of a passing good time. But ongoing satisfaction and joy from your work can come only with a loving commitment to it. "The only true happiness," said English poet William Cowper, "comes from squandering ourselves for a purpose."

Work done just for a paycheck is called making a living, surviving. But work done wholeheartedly with cheerfulness and joy, knowing you're making a difference, creates a purposeful, meaningful life. *The journey itself is the success.*

What Are Your Strengths?

As an artist, I see no reason to be egotistical about being able to draw well. I'm no better than anyone else. I just do what I've always believed I'd enjoy doing. My dynamic desire drove me to do it and become well-practiced at it; that's all.

So-called talented individuals with large egos have lost their perspective. They're just regular people like you and me, doing something very well that they, hopefully, love to do. They could be humbled by the truth that talent has a creative source much bigger than any ego-inflated feelings of self-importance.

Ego, self-focused, struts back and forth in the storefront window, while humility busily takes inventory, offers service to others, and provides the goods.

Realizing our commonality as human beings could well keep ego in check. But recognizing our uniqueness and the contributions we have to make as individuals could inspire us to expand our imaginations. We're all ordinary people in possession of extraordinary potential. Life, at its best, is the solitary discovery and unfolding of that potential, a dedication to personal development and making a difference. That's where true happiness, joy, and meaning are found.

Ditch the silly, romantic notion that "artists" (meaning anyone who's successful, no matter the field or discipline), are born as such, and don't have to develop the necessary skills. They were either born with the desire or develop it along the way—and you can count yourself among this group if you choose to do so, no matter what your desire may be.

Everyone has an aptitude to do at least one thing well. But you can only play to your strengths when you have the dynamic desire to recognize and develop them. Step outside yourself and examine, as objectively as possible, what you love and, perhaps, already do well

We're often blind to our own natural abilities or inclinations—we may overlook what comes easily to us. Even worse, we may tend to focus on our personal weaknesses, allowing any feelings of awkwardness and insecurity to define us. But why take the best in ourselves for granted?

While agreeing that each of us has a purpose for being alive, "I still don't know mine" is how many respond to that fact. People smile when I tell them everyone has the potential to do at least one thing well and with great joy. "I wish I knew what that *one thing* was," they say laughing. But wishing is only for those who get results from genies and lamp-rubbing. The rest of us need to search our soul and take action.

Think seriously about yourself. Examine your personality—the nuts and bolts of how you are as a person—and compile a list of your positive traits. What do you like about yourself? Which subjects do you enjoy learning about? What pursuits have brought you the most satisfaction in life? ("I don't know" does not qualify as a legitimate response to any of the above questions!) Be honest about it.

Take time to identify your personal strengths then commit yourself to utilizing and fine-tuning them. Nurture and develop these good qualities of yours in ways that will provide you with a more rewarding career or business of making a difference while enjoying the process. Not only is this within your power to do, it's also your responsibility.

"Why was I born?" is a common lament. Well, who, but the lamenter, is in a better position to discover the answer?

"The best is yet to come" is true only when you choose to explore the best within yourself and follow your heart.

Look at the ears of an elderly person. Notice how large they are? The cartilage which forms them continues to grow throughout life. Too bad listening skills don't always expand along with the cartilage. What's true for ears also holds true for personalities. The prominent traits we possess today will become more pronounced over time. Both sweet and sour dispositions expand with age.

What characteristics about yourself will others see accentuated in you? Kindness? Curiosity? Cheerfulness? If you haul around bitterness, impatience, or laziness, this mental baggage will really weigh you down in later years.

Assess your basic personality. Is it positive or negative? Your dominant attitude is surely a long-term investment—good or bad—in yourself.

Do We Find Ourselves or Make Ourselves?

Whenever someone tells me "I need to find myself," I endeavor to be helpful. "Have you checked between the couch cushions?" I ask. "Where was the last place you remember seeing yourself?"

Many people drift for years with the belief that their real lives will begin the moment they finally find themselves. Remember, the acorn does not search outside itself to become an oak tree!

Successful people don't waste time trying to "find" themselves; they *make* themselves as they develop their dynamic desire. It's a process of learning and growth, a daily act of creation which requires concentration, patience, and dedication to purpose or calling.

Are You Waiting for the Bus?

Imagine yourself sitting at a bus stop, miles from civilization. There you wait, but no bus comes. You stand up and begin to pace the dirt road. You're tired, hungry, and irritable. You look up the road and long for a bus to appear from over the hill, but still no bus comes. You shake your fist at the sky for being left stranded out on that road. Eventually you lose consciousness, never knowing that a bus was parked just over the hill—waiting for *you* to drive it.

What About Starving Artists?

Dreams are fragile. Without focus and dynamic desire, and the encouragement and appreciation of others, they can easily be shattered and lost forever. We may justify that loss by telling ourselves "It just wasn't meant to be. That's just the way it is."

We might think we weren't being "realistic" with our aspirations, so, just like most people, we end up settling for something less. We may stay on practical, proven paths, even though we might be sad, frustrated, or even mentally tortured by our sense of loss. After all, we may surmise, life is serious business. We've probably been taught that we need to get a good education, find a decent job, and earn enough money to live comfortably. These might have become our goals and, as a result, we've let our dreams die.

If life were a high school metal shop, a few students would strive to build bridges, but the rest would settle only for making ashtrays. How sad.

We only have a certain number of years to live and we don't know how long that will be. So why not go for the dream and start doing it now? I'm not suggesting that we ignore the responsibilities of life. But dream anyway! We can fulfill our obligations as self-reliant adults and *still* work toward living the dream.

Giving creativity free rein and allowing ourselves to believe in a dream isn't irresponsible behavior. It's just the opposite. As stated earlier, it's your duty to pursue a constructive passion. Discover, cultivate, increase, and sustain your gift of desire in a dynamic way. No one else can do it for you.

I hear a lot about "starving artists." Do you know who the real starving artists are? They're the people who deny their dreams and fail to become the best they can be. They may be earning huge sums of money; their lives may be filled with material luxuries; they may dine at only the finest restaurants, but they're starving inside. If the "artist" within you, the creative dreamer, is not permitted to grow, then a very important part of you is starving!

One of the most pleasing and happiest moments of my life came when I received the results of a personality test given to employees at the newspaper where I used to work. My answers to the battery of questions placed me under the classification, "Uncontrollable Dreamer." So why, then, had I been able to hold down a job in newspaper advertising for thirteen years, given the fact that I was an uncontrollable dreamer?

A newspaper advertising rep spends a good part of each day on the road, seeing clients, and helping them develop advertising campaigns. Not chained to a desk, I learned to work more effectively and efficiently; fulfilling the responsibilities of my job early enough to have an hour or two of free time on most days.

Through a dozen years or so in libraries and coffee shops, I used that time to read countless books, write several volumes of fiction and nonfiction, and turn my artistic abilities into a profitable career with a series of wildlife prints. Weekends were spent at juried arts and crafts festivals, evenings and early morning hours were devoted to cutting picture mats, making frames, and cutting glass.

"What you do instead of your work is your real work," said film critic, Roger Ebert.

I never shortchanged my employer, and I suggest you don't either. Strong activity management skills enabled me to develop many new accounts and set sales records, yet still have time to pursue my dreams. I didn't think much about this at the time, but the "uncontrollable dreamer" in me had naturally gravitated toward a job providing a degree of creative freedom.

Perhaps you're thinking, "Sure...it's easy to pursue your dream when you have that much free time during the day." While most people may not be in such a situation, ways can *always* be found to dedicate one or more hours to your goals daily. I'll describe some of these for you later.

Set Goals that Support Your Desires

The goals we set for ourselves need to support our desires, formulated with an understanding of our innate strengths. We all possess natural proclivities which, when nurtured and developed, can translate into a high level of proficiency and enjoyment.

If your heartfelt desire is oak trees, don't strive to create a forest of pines. "I want to win the Pulitzer Prize" is a huge goal, but taken one step at a time, could be realized. "I want to build a successful career or business, and earn a tremendous income doing so," is a great goal. "I will win an Oscar" is a great desire that can lead to becoming an accomplished actor. "I want to cure cancer" is an incredible goal, yet somebody's going to do it.

While having enthusiasm and taking action are essential for success, they're simply not enough. You need to direct these two forces into working smart, which could mean networking and associating with like-minded people. As the saying goes, "Always roll your snowballs *down*hill."

Whatever dream you choose to pursue, though, needs to provide you with an ongoing sense of accomplishment, not just a few moments of applause. When your fulfillment comes with the doing, you'll be living your dreams.

Vocation and Vision

"We can't all enjoy prestigious careers or businesses," some people have told me. "Some of us are destined to collect garbage, dig ditches, and work the assembly lines—jobs which don't exactly make your life as you would like it to be," they lament.

We often associate career or business happiness with professions that seem glamorous. People hunger for glamour because it looks attractive and exciting and easily captures their attention. But glamour is always a fluff food. Take a bite and feel it dissolve, like cotton candy, on your tongue. It can't sustain you. You need something more substantial from life's menu—something more meaningful.

Some people think a prestigious career or business is the answer to their dreams. But prestige is not synonymous with fulfillment. Would you rather be a renowned but jaded professional, who sees work as "drudgery for big bucks," or an upbeat sanitation worker who finds gratification in doing his job well? Your vision makes all the difference.

What you do always holds less significance than how you do it. A change in attitude can transform you more dramatically than can any new career or business.

People with vision see their work as an opportunity to serve. They interact with coworkers, associates, clients, and their community on a personal level, knowing that a loving outlook provides deep meaning to what they do.

"It's not how much we do that counts most," said Mother Teresa, "but with how much love we do it."

Even the humblest of tasks—such as sweeping a sidewalk—can be performed with love.

Ironically, opportunity waits at our feet as we vainly squint, looking for it on the horizon. This is especially important to remember if you're building a career or business. Such an undertaking may require years of effort before you achieve your dream.

Meanwhile, your present job or business can be viewed in a broadened, more creative context. Wherever you are today, it's likely that greater reward may be found in providing more and better service to others.

Any job or business, or any other activity for that matter, done with love, makes a positive difference. Be kind and compassionate, yet strong, in all you do. Strive to make this attitude the whole of your being, incorporating it into all that you do. This is your calling, no matter what your job or business may be, as Oliver Wendell Holmes, Jr. wrote... "Every calling is great when greatly pursued."

Now let me tell you about Sid, once a tollbooth attendant on New Jersey's Garden State Parkway. Does anyone think of such a job as glamorous? Of course not! Every day you sit in a cramped, noisy little booth, breathing exhaust fumes from the cars and trucks, taking money and giving change endlessly, all day long.

Boring, right? Well, not for Sid. His goal was to see that every driver who passed through his tollbooth left with a smile. Always upbeat, never complaining, he was genuinely interested in people, laughing and joking with them, taking time to learn a little something about their lives.

Sid seemed to know everyone. Having a problem with your car? Sid would recommend an honest mechanic. He loved helping people. If he discovered you worked locally, he might surprise you some morning by delivering a box of donuts to your office. Because he made a habit of handing out candy to kids, Sid enjoyed a wide reputation as "that great guy on the Parkway who gives stuff away."

Sid's coworkers loved him too. He always volunteered to take the busiest tollbooth lanes. He managed to find happiness in and give great joy to a job which most people would consider mundane. Significance can be found in any activity when it is performed with a loving spirit.

So What Can YOU Contribute?

"What do we live for," asked writer George Eliot, "if not to make the world less difficult for each other?"

As Oscar Hammerstein II observed, "There is a very real relationship, both quantitatively and qualitatively, between what you contribute and what you get out of this world."

Think of your life purpose, or calling, as one of creating a meaningful legacy. What can YOU contribute to those who will follow you? What talent or gift—your desire—lies within you that you can tap into and dynamically develop?

We can all be creative contributors whose work, in one form or another, will survive us to keep on giving. That's the ultimate mission to live for. It ennobles us as human beings, gives purpose and meaning to our lives, and brings happiness and joy both to ourselves and others.

People long for happiness in this life. As noted by George Bernard Shaw, "We have no more right to consume happiness without producing it, than to consume wealth without producing it."

Be a productive contributor. It's the rent we're meant to pay for the space we occupy here. Is your rent overdue? Are you current in your contributions?

What do we own? We can only claim ownership to the deeds we perform. "Actions speak louder than words" goes the sage advice.

"Well done is better than well said," wrote Benjamin Franklin. Our individual potential, acted upon in a spirit of faith and goodness, is all we really own. Actions are our possessions. They are what counts. Through them we expand beyond skin and bones to touch the lives of others and make a positive difference in the world.

Think of historical figures whose lives we admire and respect. The most influential have always been those men and women whose desire-born talents and abilities were used in service to others, weren't they? Each of us has the power to make meaningful contributions to our fellow human beings and their progeny.

Seeds of great potential have been sprinkled into our hearts. It's tragic when we don't realize this, because we won't germinate. With the flowering of what is best within us comes the deepest satisfaction and peace life can provide. Squander the opportunity and you lose sight of your purpose for being here; and the happiness and joy that could have been yours remains elusive.

Some time ago, I came upon this quote from composer Gian Carlo Menotti who managed to say, in one sentence, what I've been endeavoring to convey in the previous paragraphs: "Hell begins on the day when God grants us a clear vision of all that we might have achieved, of all the gifts which we have wasted, of all that we might have done which we did not do."

So What Will Your Epitaph Be?

Congratulations! At no cost to you or your loved ones, a bronze plaque dedicated in your memory will one day be placed in a lovely public setting where millions of people will see it. Chiseled into that plaque will be your name and a single-line epitaph to succinctly describe the way in which you lived your life. What will it say?

Which one of these epitaphs would you like to have to summarize your brief time here on earth?

- She never really lived fully.
- He settled for mediocrity because it was easy.
- She never thought of anyone but herself.
- He looked forward to the future, but never did what it took to create the life he wanted.
- "She had a big dream but never bothered to take action to make it come true.
- He was in a rut, always complaining but never changed anything.
- She never committed to anyone or anything.
- He avoided introspective thought.
- She was in a great business, but never really did what it took to build it.
- His relationships were superficial.
- She took more than she gave.
- He could have done so much more with his life.

Or could you honestly choose one of the epitaphs below as your own?

- He always did his best, then bettered it
- Her greatest satisfaction came from helping others.

- He lived in each moment and found great joy there.
- She earned great money because she contributed a lot to society.
- Money came while she worked at what she loved.
- He always dealt with people fairly and honestly.
- She loved deeply and knew the rewards of commitment.
- He knew what he wanted to accomplish and changed the world as he did it.
- His relationships were deep and abiding.
- She always gave more than she took.
- He was in a great business where he helped people all over the world, living his dream while helping others do the same.

Like it or not, your life will write its own epitaph. Would you be gratified or embarrassed to have the whole world know it?

"Inaction breeds doubt and fear. Action breeds confidence and courage. If you want to conquer fear, do not sit home and think about it. Go out and get busy."

—Dale Carnegie

"As I grow older, I pay less attention to what people say. I just watch what they do."

—Andrew Carnegie

Chapter 3
Take Action and Grow!

It's never too late to act; it's always too late not to. If you only have half a mind to do something, your other half will see to it that nothing gets done.

A good way to begin a chapter titled "Take Action and Grow!" is to return to the challenge of *inaction*. Why might taking action be so challenging for so many? Rather than living their dreams, most keep them locked up inside, doing nothing toward achieving them. Excuses may be rushing to their defense, providing cover for an unwillingness to act.

Earlier we looked at how self-limiting attitudes can hold us back from success. Now let's further examine some of the secret fears that may be responsible for chronic procrastination. Some may think or say...

"I can't possibly live my dream, so what's the use of even trying? Besides which, I'm afraid of failure. I couldn't bear the disappointment."

"So what if I *do* succeed? Then I'll always be expected to succeed from then on."

"If I fail, people will only see me as a failure. That would be humiliating."

Psychologists tell us that such fears often have their origins in childhood. Not even the best of parents can get *everything* right. Our formative years, to some degree, were probably *mal*-formative as well. Childhood insecurities, unfulfilled needs, and parental expectations may have caused us to adapt in inappropriate, self-defeating ways. Rational thinking is not the hallmark of a young child's mind, so our responses were emotional—techniques which may have served us well at the time.

Unfortunately, many remain "children" in the manner in which they cope with fear. Well-established emotional outlooks and negative thought patterns are seldom analyzed.

As adults, some might simply continue to do what worked for them as children. Instead of pursuing personal development, they may be clinging to personal *non*-development...stagnation. There might even be a certain smugness to their suffering, as they unfortunately believe that it's serving them in some way, however warped their thinking may be.

The causes for procrastination are many and often complex. "Our reasons for procrastinating are as varied as people are different," says licensed psychologist Robert B. Simmonds. He publishes an informative newsletter titled *Emotional Wellness Matters*. In Vol. 5, No. 6, he says, "...it may help to see procrastination as a symptom of underlying personality issues. For example, negative self-esteem often plays a role in our tendency to put off accomplishing tasks. Sometimes we postpone our duties because we lack self-confidence or we feel that we might be rejected by others if we don't turn in a perfect job. Sometimes procrastination is a symptom of depression."

The following stories may remind you of people in your own circle of acquaintances...or even yourself. Their names, circumstances, and many other significant details have been altered to protect their privacy. Their stories are presented to encourage your thinking about the ways in which your early life experiences may be negatively affecting your current adult behavior.

Jack was the oldest of seven children. His father, a notable professional, demanded much from him. As the first-born, Jack was expected to set a high standard of scholastic and athletic excellence for his siblings to follow. Growing up hearing very little praise from his dad, all of his efforts to excel and please him typically brought some variation of "You can always do better!" The constant pressure of never meeting his father's expectations took its toll on the boy's mental health.

Jack left home for college. Sensitive and brooding, he seemed adrift at school. Concentration on his studies was a real struggle. He turned to alcohol and spent most of his time watching TV in the student lounge. Placed on academic probation, he did nothing to change his behavior and eventually dropped out.

Telling Jack to contemplate his tremendous potential would have sent him into a panic. With greater achievement, Jack feared that pressures to perform at a higher level would grow. Life would be too demanding. "Who needs that kind of stress?" he said. Jack's fear of success effectively immobilized him. Failure, for him, provided a form of relief.

Diane was intelligent and attractive, but terribly insecure. She felt uncomfortable making any decision alone. Her dependence on others' advice and opinions began early.

Diane's father was a chronic philanderer, often absent from home. Her mother, unwilling to divorce and break up the family, directed all love and attention toward Diane, the only child. She was domineering, involved in every aspect of her daughter's life. Not even Diane's clothing and hairstyle decisions were made without parental consultation.

Diane's compliance and passivity won her mother's praise and approval, but these success-thwarting attributes trapped her into being a young woman distrustful of her own opinions. Feelings of inadequacy even poisoned her potential romantic relationships.

Whenever a man showed interest, Diane distanced herself, acting out a version of the famous Groucho Marx line, "I'd never join a club that would have *me* as a member." For Diane, the feeling was, "Why should I respect anyone who finds *me* lovable?"

People, like Diane, who feel unworthy or inadequate, react to the claim, "You have great potential," with disbelief. To them, it's farfetched. They simply won't accept it. Within them dwells the constant fear, "I don't have what it takes. I'm not good enough."

Ted worked far below his creative and intellectual potential, in a routine job he performed exceptionally well. He often complained that his work didn't challenge him, but when opportunities for advancement came his way, he always passed them up. Why did he, probably unconsciously, choose to stay stuck?

Ted's childhood was lonely. An emotionally disturbed younger brother received most of his parents' attention, leaving Ted feeling unimportant. "They seemed to take for granted that I could handle myself without much help," he said. So he withdrew emotionally, creating a macho image façade of total self-assurance.

As an adult, Ted continued to wear this mask. He wasn't a risk-taker. Though bright and witty, he hunkered down in an efficient mediocrity. This may have been unfulfilling, but at least Ted felt he was in control. He hated his work, but he did it meticulously.

For Ted, personal development was too great a gamble. To step outside of what he did perfectly would expose his vulnerability. Since he believed that he might be criticized or attacked for his actions, he chose to stay positioned behind his armor of capability, despite the accompanying boredom and unhappiness. Personal growth for Ted meant the surrender of his long-standing fortress.

If you feel stuck then the way you currently conduct your life is providing some kind of payoff or you wouldn't continue doing what you're doing. Security at all costs? Fear avoidance? Approval from others? Familiarity of the status quo?

Imagine the worst that could happen if you actually *moved toward* your dream. "Do the things you fear" isn't just good advice for the conquering of mild phobias. It's also an excellent way—in fact, the *only* way—to make positive changes in your life.

Do you harbor any long-standing fears? If so, do you realize they can slam the door on your personal development, closing you off from a world of promise and possibility? Return to the observer approach described in *Chapter One.* "Catch yourself in the act" when you experience emotional, child-responses to fear.

Exploring those feelings will position you to make affirmative changes in attitude and behavior. You grow by first understanding any immature accommodations to fears that you may have developed, followed by establishing new, more mature approaches to living.

This can be a challenging task but the payoffs to such positive change—personal freedom and fulfillment—are your rewards for committed effort. If, for some reason, you experience some backsliding, just pick up where you left off and go at it again.

In pursuing any worthwhile goal, "We need to separate our emotions from the task itself," writes Dr. Simmonds. "In fact, working at the task gives us a good opportunity to see what our emotions are and to confront them honestly.

"This then allows us to learn where the feelings are coming from so that we can resolve them. Avoiding painful feelings lets them linger on into the future, but confronting them, especially with the help of a supportive and insightful therapist, can lead to emotional liberation."

We may look at certain people and say, "Wow! He (or she) has it all together." But life is paradoxical. In truth, those who basically have it all together understand and accept that parts of themselves will *always* be at loose ends. That's the universal human condition. Everyone is a mixed bag of strengths and weaknesses. Virtually all of us feel vulnerable in some areas. No matter how anyone may appear to be above it all, no one really is.

When you understand personal development is a natural, exciting ongoing lifetime process which you are equipped to handle, you will be on you way to developing your dynamic desire. That, to borrow a movie title, is "as good as it gets."

How Do You Value Time?

You've heard the expression, "Time marches on," and it certainly does that and more. Time dashes by…so use it wisely! Sometimes it may seem that the inner neck of life's hourglass has been sprayed with some sort of lubricant. Those grains of sand fall through so quickly.

Life gives us only a guest room for the weekend, yet some of us live as if we owned the house. Well, obviously, we're not permanent residents here. The good news is that, while we're made of clay, we can sculpt ourselves into works of art.

"Everything comes to him who hustles while he waits," said Thomas Edison. Time is our most precious commodity, yet many of us don't utilize it very well. Time is opportunity and squandered opportunity is a "club," unfortunately, whose membership is way too large.

Rudyard Kipling said, "Fill the unforgiving minute with 60 seconds worth of distance run."

My dad was an English teacher. He liked to give his seventh-grade students a thought for the day. One of his favorites was the old Russian proverb, "A falling leaf is a whisper to the living."

Look around. Nature's design of us humans could be thought of as "planned obsolescence," as we're all going to die. We just don't know when! But how many of us thoughtfully plan our lives with a sense of importance and urgency?

What if, all of a sudden, Father Time tapped you on the shoulder and said, "Your time is about up. You have only a year to live"? What is it you long to do before you die? What dreams would you like to fulfill? What goals would you like to accomplish? What have you been meaning to do?

In the long-run, we learn that life is really a 50-yard dash. When the dust settles, we're all dust. What will have been your contribution to life? What will be your legacy left to grow? What would you like it to be?

Shakespeare was right—"Our time upon the stage is but an hour." In those precious moments we can:

- Strut and fret.
- Complain about the lighting.
- Paralyze ourselves with stage fright.
- Worry that we'll bump into the furniture.
- Obsess over our make-up.
- Continue to rehearse behind the curtain.
- Refuse to go on until we get a bigger dressing room.
- Stand in the wings and envy other actors.
- Allow ourselves to be strung and used as marionettes, or
- Do something else nonproductive.

We can also choose to walk directly into the spotlight and deliver a solid, memorable performance. What will you do on the stage of your life?

Time Is a Most Precious Treasure

Consider the short span of your life in the immensity of all time and you may feel you are insignificant. But the here-and-now of a lifetime is the only time that truly exists in which desires can be worked toward and realized; and within this "moment" your contribution can be significant.

The continual sweep of the second-hand turns all our moments in to dust. What remains of anyone, ultimately, are the positive or negative effects of his or her actions.

"One day, I'll find the time." Have you ever said that? Well, you needn't search for it. The time is here and now. It's staring you in the face. What will you do with it? In the game of life, it's always your move.

I've always been keenly aware of the passage of time—too much so, actually. I'll tell you a secret. When I was in college, I used to go to the library and leaf through books of early photography. I was drawn to studying 100-year-old photographs of crowd scenes, Victorian men and women strolling along the boardwalk, marching in parades, or gathering under tents for revival meetings. I studied pictures of people who were full of dreams and desires, people that were no different than you and I, except they were gone. All of them. Dust.

I wondered what they did with their lives after the camera captured their images on film. What did they give to life? Who had they helped along the way?

I saw another old photograph recently when I stopped at a bagel shop for breakfast. While waiting at the counter, I noticed a large poster on the back wall. It pictured the interior of a train station. Printed beneath the photograph, in capital letters, was the caption, "GRAND CENTRAL STATION, 1934." The shot had been taken from above, looking at the rush of people below as they made their way through the station. Shafts of afternoon sunlight from high windows shone down on the tiny figures, bathing them in a soft glow.

The scene had a special look. Caught on film in that long ago instant was an ephemeral quality, a feeling of sweet sadness. These people with all their plans, carried along by the hurried pace of daily living, didn't seem to notice what the photographer may have well understood: the almost mysteri-

ous beauty and fragile, fleeting nature of that particular moment—and of all the moments of our lives.

Studying photographs of people gone long before I was
born, I became more aware of the continuity of life. We all
have a part to play. Today, and all the days of our lives, it's
always our turn to move forward.

What difference can you make while you're here? Answer that question, and then take your first step to act on it.
Someday, someone may look at an old photograph of you
and think, "What did this person do with his or her life?"

In Thornton Wilder's play, *Our Town*, a young woman,
Emily, dies and is given the opportunity to return and observe any single day of her short life. When Emily wants to
relive an especially happy day, she's told, "Choose an unimportant day. Choose the least important day in your life. It
will be important enough."

Emily returns to a day from childhood and finds that she
"can't look at everything hard enough." She's overwhelmed
by the beauty of it all. "I can't go on," she says. "It goes so
fast. We don't have time to look at one another." Emily discovers profound meaning in the smallest of moments, and
she begins to cry. "I didn't realize...all that was going on
and...I never noticed."

Late in his life, Thornton Wilder wrote that *Our Town*
was his "attempt to find a value above all price for the smallest events in our daily life." Imagine how much richer your
life would be if you could hold in your mind the inestimable
worth of each of your moments here on earth. Time viewed
as treasure would not be so casually spent.

Director Frank Capra's 1946 film, *It's a Wonderful Life*, is
one of my favorites. It's a great story. A near-suicidal George
Bailey, played by Jimmy Stewart, is given a chance to see
what life in his hometown would've been like had he never
been born. George learns all the positive ways in which his
actions influenced the people he knew. Without his caring

presence on the stage of life, the lives of relatives, friends, and acquaintances were altered dramatically, and not for the better.

This thought-provoking movie can be a revelation to everyone. Each of us touches the lives of more people in more ways than he or she realizes. Even the smallest acts of kindness have a ripple effect which can reach countless others. So simple a gesture as a loving smile at the right moment may alter the life course of a stranger's life!

This isn't wishful thinking. It's a glimpse at the awesome power each of us holds, moment to moment, to do either good or ill. Like Thornton Wilder's character Emily, George Bailey comes to understand and value the profound meaning of all the moments of daily living. *It's a Wonderful Life* reveals the truth that life well lived is a wondrous process of learning to see and understand, in glorious detail, what is in our immediate view. Each decent action or honorable choice you make is a test-flight of your soul's wings.

Have Your Ever Thought About the Underside of a Leaf?

When I give a motivational talk, I ask the people in the audience to complete an evaluation form at the conclusion of the presentation. Their comments and suggestions guide me to provide more helpful information in future programs.

During my talks, I refer to the brevity of life. This usually prompts at least one person to write the following on his or her evaluation sheet: "Inspirational message, but too much talk about death."

While only a few minutes of my program deal with the subject of mortality, some think that's a few minutes too many! Now, I'm not a morbid guy. My eventual demise is not a thought I like to dwell on. But our acceptance of our mortality can be a great gift to ourselves. It can awaken us and prod us to set meaningful priorities. A healthy appreciation that our life will end can inspire us to realize more of life's possibilities.

Many years ago, the wife of a former Senator was stricken with terminal cancer. She wrote eloquently about living with the disease. One poignant comment in particular stays with me: "Only after being diagnosed with cancer did I discover the beauty of the underside of a leaf." With the threat of impending death, she awoke to the miracle of life and really began to see.

Your heightened awareness of life's majesty and mystery needn't wait for your closing days. Facing the reality of your ultimate death today can enhance the meaning of all your tomorrows.

Now Is the Time to Act—*What Are You Waiting For?*

As a kid, I had the good fortune to have my great-grandmother live with us. I grew up under the same roof with a woman born in the 1870s. She was still alive and well in the 1970s. Her life spanned eras from the horse and buggy to lunar landings. It was a good, long life, yet even she was amazed by how quickly the years slipped away.

Living with someone that old was a blessing, because it shrank history for me. I realized, at an early age, that, even when you're here for a relatively long time in terms of human existence, you're not really here for a very long time. Life comes one day at a time, but the days seem to bunch together as we grow older. So get busy! Just because we come from dust and will someday return to dust, does not mean we need to be gathering dust while we're here.

How often do you catch yourself or others saying, "Someday, I'll...."? Forget it! For far too many, "someday" becomes a new word called "never" and they die with their song unsung, their potential unfulfilled. I think of someday as a lifetime calendar with all the months and days missing.

No one stands the test of time by remaining seated, a spectator in front of the TV. You can't make a deep impression on others while making a deep impression on your couch. "This is a world of action," said Charles Dickens, "and not for moping and droning in." We're creatures limited only by time and how we use it. Forget about what you're going to do someday. What are you doing today?

Good intentions alone can't accomplish anything. They are pleasant thoughts left to fade and be forgotten. Not acted upon, they let time flit away. It's useless to talk about a desired outcome if you're not diligently working toward it. Otherwise, it's just so much hot air.

Remember, there's always room at the top, but you can't get there sitting on your bottom. If you think you can do a thing, you can do it—unless all you do is *think* about doing it, in which case you can't. *Positive thinking without positive action is only wishful thinking.* Wishful thinking is all dressed up with no place to go.

All things begin in the brain, but don't let them end there. Wishes wobble in place. Only positive actions can advance!

In elementary school, we learned that a noun is a person, place, or thing. A noun is a person? How boring it is to be placed in the same category as a slab of concrete or a clump of sod! Let's think of ourselves as *verbs*—always in motion and taking positive action.

Making something more of your life requires movement, or why have arms and legs? Our bodies are comprised mostly of water. What happens when a body of water stops moving? Algae grows unabated, it gets stale and polluted, starts smelling bad and looking ugly, and breeds mosquitoes. So get moving! Live your life as a verb, *an italicized underlined verb!* Develop your dynamic desire as you move forward.

Get Off Your Assets—*Success Doesn't Offer Home Delivery*

Have you ever known people who thought their talents were obvious, believing that opportunities would seek them out? One day, success would surely fall into their laps without any effort on their part. But since they park themselves in front of the TV every night the only things to fall into their laps are pretzel, potato chip, and cookie crumbs.

Don't expect to be picked up and carried on the shoulders of success if you're sitting comfortably with the TV remote in your hand. Get off your assets!

During the Golden Age of Hollywood, stories were circulating about pretty young women, while bagging groceries in small town markets, being discovered by talent scouts. The movie industry whisked them away and made them stars. But those days are pretty much over; and even if that isn't so, you need to act as if it were. The world is much too busy to take notice of how wonderful you are as you just sit there, or go about your normal routine, not doing anything above average.

It seems obvious that getting where you want to go in life starts by moving from where you currently are. We all know people, though, who want to reach their desired destination without bothering to make the trip. We hear them dream, scheme, and idly talk about where they long to be, as though this wishful thinking could somehow uproot the goal or dream and powerfully haul it to their present location.

Success doesn't offer home delivery. Would those who think success comes automatically ever expect food for next week's meals to make its own way into their refrigerators?

"Lights! Camera! Inaction!" A director would never yell this command on a movie set. The cost of poor or nonuse of actor and crew time would be exorbitant. Procrastination would shut down production. No one will use a bullhorn to tell you, but the lights of possibility in your life are on and your days are rolling. You can't afford to mill around on the set; the cost is way too high. You're allotted only a limited time for production. Use it wisely.

Continue Learning, Growing, and Taking Positive Action

Many of us tend to pack away our learning skills along with our diplomas and degrees. Become a lifetime student of personal development and all of life will be a supportive teacher. You don't have to spend a lifetime with yourself just as you are. Education and motivation enable you to choose better company.

In the same way that you can't bake a great cake without the right ingredients, neither can you achieve a goal without the right knowledge. Immerse yourself in your subject of interest and study every aspect of it. You're doing more than simply acquiring information. All those facts and insights "bake" inside your brain, forming new thoughts, helping you focus and develop the dynamic desire necessary to propel you toward reaching your goals and dreams.

Build a foundation of research and new understanding. You can benefit from the knowledge of experts and those who've achieved the goal or dream you desire. Observe, listen to, talk to, and associate with people who are successful doing what you're endeavoring to accomplish.

Learn from the great minds that came before you. Read! Their knowledge, wisdom, and experiences are yours to learn from and emulate. That's their gift to you. Don't let it grow dusty in a library, on your own bookshelf, or stuck in your computer or mobile device. Utilize it.

"If a man empties his purse into his head," said Ben Franklin, "no one can take it away from him. An investment in knowledge always pays the best interest."

Taking in ideas that are new to you stimulates your mind to think more creatively. Interact with what you read. Think about and realize what you're learning, then decide for yourself how to best apply and make it work going forward. Then get moving!

The creation of a wholly original idea is virtually impossible. Genius doesn't explode upon the scene from nowhere. What is viewed as original thought generally arises from the reworking of earlier thoughts in new and improved ways. Brilliance, cleverness, and innovation aren't usually brought about by "a-bolt-from-the-blue" inspiration—although it can start this way, it typically doesn't.

Chances are, if you postpone action until you feel inspired, you've taken a permanent seat in life's waiting room. The only two times you need to do something is when you feel like it and, more importantly, when you don't!

In what subject would you like to experience a stroke of genius? Study it deeply, until you become a wealth of knowledge. You'll discover the truth concerning genius. Neither glamorous nor original, it takes place when we accumulate borrowed thoughts, then blow the dust off them by refashioning them in innovative ways.

"I am more of a sponge than an inventor," said Thomas Edison. "I absorb ideas from every source. My principal business is giving commercial value to the brilliant but misdirected ideas of others."

Creativity is driven by your desire, the more dynamic the better, and increases with the imaginative use of that which already exists. Acquired knowledge, written in our own unique handwriting, that is, from our own individual perspective, creates "original" thought.

I usually describe myself as a self-taught artist, but this is somewhat inaccurate. No one is ever really self-taught. I've learned from every artist whose work I observed or admired as I had the desire to do so. Instructional art books, art galleries, and museums have provided me with tools as essential as the paper and pencils I used to practice and sharpen my skills.

Your originality will emerge with the intelligent use of your time and effort. While the adage "There's nothing new under the sun" is true, your imagination can alter the lighting in new and beautiful ways.

You *Can* Enrich and Extend Your Life

Most of us want to live longer, right? We exercise, do our best to eat the right foods, and take vitamin and mineral supplements. This can certainly improve the quality of our lives—and maybe even add many years. But can we expect to double or triple our life spans? Perhaps not, although this may change as new longevity studies are conducted and health-enhancing innovations are made. But it is possible to "extend" life in another way.

While you may not be able to add years to your life, you can add more life to your years... and enrich it by looking back and learning from the great achievers. In a very real sense, books can be your personal time machine, transporting you to other eras and places where you can meet accomplished people who cared enough to put thoughts and ideas into permanent form for your benefit. What a wonderful legacy they've given you. Virtually all the genius this world has ever produced is available for you to tap into, learn from, and use for your benefit.

Keep learning the ideas of great minds. Your own mind will continue to expand as you add centuries of breadth and depth to your life. Avail yourself of all the great teachers and leaders this world provides—both past and present.

I'm thankful for those precious, dynamic desire-driven people whose words have touched my life and helped to point the way for me to gain greater understanding and accomplish more of what is on my heart to do. Dip into this vast reservoir of knowledge and wisdom and drink from it daily. You'll be amazed by the number of different ways in which your life is inspired, empowered, and changed for the better.

Turn off the TV and read. Abraham Lincoln is whispering, "Spend an evening with me." Anne Morrow Lindbergh is tapping you on the shoulder, "I have something to tell you." Dale Carnegie is saying, "Listen to me and you'll have greater success." Og Mandino is asking, "Have you read my parables?"

The list of people whose words can enrich and extend your life is endless and constantly growing. Begin to enhance your life. Consider the words of esteemed speaker and best-selling author the late Charlie "Tremendous" Jones, "The only difference between where you are now and where you'll be in the next five years will be the people you meet and the books you read."

Remove a Key Roadblock to Action

If you think you might look silly doing something new, just say to yourself, "Who cares?" With that kind of attitude, you free yourself up to master almost anything.

Unfortunately, some people's egos transform them into large, concrete barriers, blocking their road to personal growth. Could this be true for you?

Most of us are reluctant to appear clumsy or awkward in any new venture. Self-consciousness may prevent us from accepting the fact that beginners generally look that way. It's simply the nature of starting anything new.

"A thing worth doing," wrote G.K. Chesterton, "is worth doing badly." It's fine to set a high standard for yourself, but it's quite unrealistic to expect the instant attainment of that standard. Patient acceptance of steady growth, which may seem slow at times, is needed. Along with that, the ability to use failure and frustration as fuel to feed your desire is essential for you to keep moving forward.

The idea of unlocking your creative potential can be intimidating if you compare yourself to experts whose work or accomplishments you admire. That's not comparing apples to apples. It's comparing apple seeds to apples! We forget that great artists, writers, business people, musicians—experts in every field—began by first doing it badly and persisting until they became proficient at it.

As a child with an insatiable curiosity, you demonstrated a comfortable awkwardness, while learning from the world around you, which led to your doing new things. Since you did it once back then, YES, you can do it again now!

Muster Some Courage and Be Adventurous!

It can be challenging to alter your old everyday boring course of action and follow a new and exciting path that can help you work toward realizing more of your potential—like entering an unfamiliar room, perhaps in total darkness. Naturally, you'd expect to bump into some furniture, so a little bit of courage and a sense of adventure is in order. In the face of some risk you also need to have some faith. Be confident as you move forward, and accept that your shins may get bruised. No big deal.

Keep a playful attitude as you feel your way around the new situation. Become familiar with the surroundings at your own pace, and with this knowledge your confidence will grow. Remember, no courage is needed where there is no fear. Taking positive action is always the best cure for overcoming fear.

"Dis" is an innocent-sounding, unhealthy little prefix I found in the dictionary. In Latin, it means "apart, to pieces." Today we tack it onto the front of words to signify (1) reverse, (2) deprive of, (3) expel from, or (4) absence of.

Remember "dis" if you ever allow yourself to become *dis*couraged, then *discard* it!

In the same dictionary, I also found a healthy prefix, "en." What a powerful combination of two letters! It can mean (1) put on, (2) cause to be, (3) provide with, or (4) cover or surround thoroughly.

Let that *en*courage you!

Knowledge and Opportunity Call for Action

"Knowing is not enough;" said the German poet Goethe, "we must apply. Willing is not enough; we must do." He also said, "Whatever you can do or dream, you can begin it. Boldness has genius, power, and magic in it."

We've all heard the expression, "Knowledge is power." But is that really true? Knowledge can't do anything by itself. Only when you act on it will knowledge hold any power for you. Knowledge is fuel, but you still need to start the engine of action.

While we're blowing clichés out of the water, let's take aim at another one: "Be ready when opportunity knocks." But does opportunity *really* knock? I guarantee you it won't appear at your front door with balloons and a certified check. No bells, no whistles, no fanfare.

Opportunity never knocks, but it's always there—waiting for *you* to knock and take advantage of. It isn't glamorous either. Thomas Edison is one of my heroes, so I quote him often. "Opportunity," he said, "is missed by most people because it's dressed in overalls and looks like work." There's nothing romantic about it.

Make Time for Your Dream...Stop Spectating and Start Participating in Creating a Brighter Future!

"I'm working a full-time job. I don't like the way things are going, but there aren't enough hours in the day as it is, let alone time to pursue my dream."

This is a common lament or complaint, but simply unacceptable for anyone who's truly serious about their future happiness and success. It's really just an excuse that keeps people stuck! If everyone bought into that line of so-called reasoning, no one would ever accomplish much of anything beyond working a job or doing the other ordinary things of life.

According to recent surveys, on average, people spend around 20 hours a week watching TV, online and off, and nearly 12 hours a week checking their five social media accounts, distracting themselves from a life they're simply not passionate about. Could that be what you're doing as well?

If you're even the least bit unhappy with your life situation, why not restructure your routine and change your habits to better utilize your time by pursuing your cherished dream? How many of those hours could you utilize in working toward it, or a "Someday I'll..." goal, perhaps by building your own business outside of working your job?

How about using your social media accounts more productively as a tool for building your own business? Instead of wasting time watching the negative news, which can be quite a downer, why not use that 30 or 60 minutes to better your life?

What's the point of watching TV shows, mindlessly observing actors living *their* dream, portraying fictional characters, when you could be investing that time in creating a better life for you and your family...*so you can live your own dream*? Doesn't that make sense?

Another time-consumer is lunch. Fortunately, for example, you can simultaneously eat and read some educational or business information, so five lunch hours every week could be devoted toward increasing your knowledge.

Set your alarm clock fifteen minutes earlier than usual, and invest that time in reading a positive, uplifting book. It can help keep you on track and inspire you to take action. Focus on subject matter associated with what you want to achieve—perhaps a personal or professional development book. Do this for a month, until it becomes routine, then set your alarm back another fifteen minutes. Continue this practice over a period of several months until you have a full hour of early morning time devoted to creating a better life.

Twenty hours no longer spent watching TV, plus five lunch hours, plus seven quiet early morning hours, and 12 hours of non-productive checking of social media... gives you a total of 44 hours weekly that you could dedicate toward achieving your dream or goal. That's the equivalent of over five workdays a week invested in pursuing what you long to do.

The bottom line is that you DO *have the time to create a brighter future. So, make it a priority!*

Maybe this seems unrealistic to you, given your personal circumstances. Okay, let's assume that's true. Tell me you can't find, in your daily schedule, at least 60 minutes you could be using more wisely. Locate just 60 minutes, the time it takes to watch just one TV show. Be totally honest with yourself. Most people waste or poorly use at least that much time every day, and usually A LOT more.

Take those 60 minutes and reserve them exclusively for your personal and professional development. Guard that time from interruptions, and never skip a day, especially if you don't feel like doing it. Dedicate yourself in doing so the same time, every day. This is a mark of a winner!

"How much can I possibly get done in 60 minutes?" you may be asking. Perhaps not a lot; however, what could you accomplish with 21,900 minutes, which is 365 hours? That string of hours represents over 45 eight-hour workdays. This is what one year of following a modest, 60-minute daily schedule change gives you. That's plenty of developmental time to help you toward pursuing your dreams and goals. You may not think you're gifted, but you *do* have your desire, don't you? So... how dynamic is it?

Do you commute to and from work? Pop a motivational, personal development, continuing education, or instructional audio into your player and turn your car into a "university on wheels." Absorb creative ideas every day to break your old routine. Listening to an audio every day is a good habit to get into. You'll be using those precious hours to help you become whatever you desire. Listen to them over and over again to be sure you hear and retain what is important to you. It's said that we need to listen to a message at least six times before we get a reasonable understanding of it.

Each of us is an architect. Any worthwhile endeavor begins with proper planning. Angry, bitter, disillusioned people are often those who see no need for blueprints. They just sort of let things happen, like a ship without a rudder.

While few people are in a position to make an abrupt change in their career or job, it's always possible to make life changes slowly. How many of us can honestly say that 100 percent of a typical day is being used productively? Most of us use some of our time unwisely. Take those valuable hours and discipline yourself to devote them to the gradual attainment of your desire.

Research, study, and develop a plan whereby you can gradually shift your energies from one endeavor to another. Ask for help, as this can be challenging. It requires self-sustaining drive and the desire to stay on course. Ask for support as you need it. Maintain a strong commitment to moving forward. Begin with the belief that there's always a way, and with persistent focus and effort, you'll eventually find it. If, for some reason, one way doesn't work out, you'll find another.

"Whether you're flying the Atlantic or selling sausages," said Amelia Earhart, "building a skyscraper or driving a truck, your greatest power comes from the fact that you want tremendously to do that very thing, and do it well." So, whatever your goal is, to build a career or business, or something else, it all starts with desire. That's the gift, pure and simple.

Find a Mentor—*If There's a Shortcut to Success, This Is It*

I was working as a newspaper account executive when I first decided to learn the business side of being an artist. A fellow salesman offered to introduce me to his brother-in-law, Frank Hulick, a full-time professional in the field.

An accomplished wildlife artist, Frank not only took time to critique my artwork and offer encouragement, but also steered me to the best wholesale source for mats, glass, and other art supplies. He shared information about lucrative art shows and festivals, and where to send for applications.

His advice was priceless. By openly sharing this knowledge, Frank made the business of art a less intimidating prospect for me. He really smoothed the road. My goal to be a full-time artist was realized, in no small way, because of Frank's kind, thoughtful assistance. He's a natural mentor. I've spoken with numerous people who feel the same way about him. Frank has helped so many others to realize their dreams.

Find a mentor. Seek out people who are successful in your field of interest. Offer to take them to breakfast or lunch. Be honest. Tell them you need direction, you respect them and what they've accomplished, and could benefit from their expertise. Some will be generous with their wisdom and life experiences. (Though I never invited Frank to breakfast or lunch, my wife did bake a delicious apple cake for him!) Watch, listen, and learn from them—and do what they did to get where they are.

Be sure to ask these people how they've handled failure and rejection. What would they do differently, given the opportunity to start over? Create a list of such questions before meeting your potential mentors. Successful caring people enjoy sharing their wisdom and experiences to help others. Listen and learn from what they share with you.

My wife's dream had long been to own and manage a bed-and-breakfast. Jan stayed in many inns before opening one of her own. In those inns, she found many mentors. Once the breakfast dishes were cleared away, most innkeepers were happy to share their personal stories with her.

"What don't you like about this business?" was usually Jan's first question. "Lack of privacy," was a common complaint from innkeepers, and an important factor to keep in mind when searching for an old home with bed-and-breakfast potential. Those gracious innkeepers provided invaluable information, enabling her to enter the profession with her eyes wide open. She gained a broad knowledge of and some valuable insights about the business, while discussing it with me, getting my support, and welcoming her first guest.

Be especially courteous to your mentors. When successful people take time from their busy schedules for you, follow up with a note of thanks for their kindness. Show your appreciation.

Feline Wisdom

We live with three cats. In addition to the companionship and affection they provide, these fascinating creatures are also good teachers. Cats live wisely. Here are ten lessons we can all learn from them:

1. **Begin each day in an upbeat mood.** Cats always get up in a positive frame of mind. They awaken ready to explore the world (or at least their small part of it).

2. **Develop your powers of concentration.** A cat can achieve perfect focus. Watch one when it sights a bird or squirrel. A powerful concentration takes over and the rest of the world disappears.

3. **Be courageous and take a leap.** Cats always jump with confidence. They'll leap distances many times their own height to get to where they want to go.

4. **Occasionally take a detached view.** Cats find a high perch from which to quietly observe their surroundings. People could benefit by doing the same.

5. **See value in imaginative play.** Even a simple piece of string or a paper bag, approached playfully, provides cats great exercise for both mind and body. They use play to "stay loose."

6. **Realize the importance of rest and relaxation.** While I don't recommend their sleep schedule (16 hours a day), cats do know how to relax and find joy in the moment. They handle stress well.

7. **Be patient.** If they wait long enough on a windowsill, cats know something of interest will come into view.

8. **Clean up after yourself.** We don't need to go into detail about this one. Let's just say that cats take responsibility for their own messes.

9. **Be yourself.** Like people, cats are sometimes slightly zany. (They get that way from living with us!) One moment your cat is sitting quietly on the couch. Suddenly, the fur on its back starts to twitch. The cat stares at you wildly, then darts from the room for no apparent reason. (If you choose to mimic this behavior, do so only around people who know you really well.) Cats accept the streak of irrationality within themselves.

10. **Don't take yourself *too* seriously.** This is the message cats try to convey whenever they roll onto their backs and look at us upside-down. They remind us to lighten up a bit.

"*Some people think that I've had an easy time of it. They say I have 'the Hershey luck,' whatever that is, and as a result money flowed into my lap.*

"But luck had nothing to do with my success...my success is the result of not being satisfied with mediocrity, and in making the most of my opportunities."

—Milton S. Hershey

Chapter 4
Exercise Discipline and Persevere

*People often become successful long before their names
or deeds are known. The transformation occurs the moment they pledge their heart, mind, and spirit, affirming,
"I'm committed to achieving my goals and dreams."*

One of my favorite quotes is from Henry David Thoreau, and it was super-easy to memorize. He advised,
"Simplify, simplify, simplify."

Life wants to interrupt you sixty times an hour to ask,
"Got a minute?" There are many ways the world can distract
you. Life has a way of pulling you in a dozen different directions...*but only if you let it.*

Be determined to stay on track. Concentrate. Practice discipline and self-denial. All are required for success and
deeply intertwined with another essential element... perseverance. Furthermore, as Sir Walter Scott said, "Teach self-
denial and make its practice pleasure, and you can create for
the world a destiny more sublime than ever issued from the
brain of the wildest dreamer."

Focus your attention and energies on your desire and
stay determined to accomplish your goals. Otherwise, you

won't get what you want. It's hard to orchestrate your life if you've scattered your sheet music throughout the theater.

Running to and fro, people often weave and dodge their way around moments they have every day to do something toward accomplishing their desire. "There's so much I should be doing," they lament, "but I just don't know where to begin." They walk in circles, scattered, fearful, getting nowhere, unwilling to make their desire a priority, for whatever reason or excuse, unproductively using their time until their complaint ultimately becomes an unwritten epitaph.

Efficient, effective, productive, proactive people know a lot of low-priority things on their list will never get done, but that's okay as these things just aren't very important in the achievement of their goals or dreams. They've learned what to retain, what to eliminate, and what to delegate.

This kind of streamlined attention to their desire brings to mind the artwork of the late Al Hirschfeld, whose delightful drawings chronicled the New York theater scene—and all the performing arts—since the early 1920s. He was a master of the art of caricature. His witty portraits focused on what was most distinctive about a person, eliminating all unnecessary detail. With just a few, well-placed lines and curves, Hirschfeld not only delineated a performer's likeness, but also defined the heart of that person's character.

His drawings took either hours or days to complete. His theatrical sketches captured a stage filled with movement, compressing all that activity onto a sheet of paper. "A magic takes place" is how Hirschfeld described his technique.

He became a visual translator of the playwright's intentions, freezing emotion and mood with an economy of line. Simple loops and swirls infused his art with a current of energy. "Mouths became caverns, slits," he said. "Hair might be Brillo, rope, string, thread."

Hirschfeld's imagination cut through the extraneous, leaving only the essence of features and personality. But each remaining line was crucial to the composition. He excelled in the art of simplification, his economy of line producing drawings full of playful humor, causing me to smile every time I see one.

Take what Al Hirschfeld did with his pen and apply it to your personal goals. You write your own script in life, and the greatest fulfillment comes to those who practice good editing. As bestselling author Mario Puzo said, "The secret to writing is rewriting."

You can't sign up for every course of interest when your life lasts only one semester. So pick and choose carefully, as tomorrow is promised to no one.

Keep Hirschfeld's drawings in mind. Cut through extraneous details. Simplify and focus on what's essential to cultivating your own gift—your desire.

Success Is Found in Overcoming Challenges

Here's another favorite Thoreau quote of mine. "If one advances confidently in the direction of his dreams and endeavors to live the life which he has imagined, he will meet with a success unexpected in common hours."

Being confident and optimistic about your dreams is effortless when your life is going well and you see tangible evidence of progress toward a goal. At these times, faith in yourself is as natural as blinking and breathing.

The real test comes if you run into some major obstacles and no one is there who believes in you and what you're doing. Even your dog seems aloof.

If such periods of time come, and they may, your confidence and faith are given an opportunity to become more than mere words that make you feel warm and cozy. They can support and guide you, pushing you forward, defining both your character and the substance of your desire.

Football coach Vince Lombardi said, "It's easy to have faith in yourself and have discipline when you're a winner, when you're number one. What you've got to have is faith and discipline when you're *not* [yet] a winner."

Success is achieved in overcoming the challenges. "Lasting accomplishment," said actress Helen Hayes, "is achieved through a long, slow climb and self-discipline." Successful people often say jokingly that it takes 15 years to become an overnight success. So give yourself time to succeed.

As discussed, we are born with the capacity to believe in ourselves and have the faith that our lives hold purpose. Otherwise, we disparage our desire, born with it or developed.

If you don't experience more challenges than comforts in life, you're not really stretching and growing. Genius is usually the romantic name we give to thoughtful endurance.

If things always came up smelling like roses, the scent would soon go unnoticed. People usually take for granted whatever comes to them easily. It's our hard, and smart, work in dealing with challenges that gives us a true appreciation for what we've earned. They bring value to our goals. Since challenges met and overcome strengthen and move us forward, why not welcome them? You do want to grow stronger, don't you?

Learning how to lift the weight of challenges from our shoulders tones and develops who we are. Think of challenges as exercise equipment for the mind. Obstacles are an integral part of any life well lived.

Wherever you live, Challenge may always be the "neighbor" who stops in without phoning first. Open the door for him or her. To pretend you're not "home" is to ignore Challenge and choose not to grow; therefore not to achieve your goals and dreams. The greatest natural resource available to you is the power of your mind to address, and then take action to overcome life's challenges. That which is best within you can be discovered and mined in no other way.

"The great crisis must come," said Theodore Roosevelt, "or no man has the chance to develop great qualities."

You're Fired!

Several years ago, radio talk-show host Rush Limbaugh opened his phone lines to people who had been forced to change careers in mid-life. He wanted to hear how they had used this challenging event as a springboard to greater success. Limbaugh thought it was crucial to provide listeners with a positive alternative to the whining victims continually presented to us by the mainstream media. America, argued Limbaugh, was still the best place to fulfill a dream, and he wanted his callers to prove it.

What followed was the most inspiring three hours of radio I've ever heard. People phoned in with incredible stories of overcoming personal setbacks. Some detailed painful hardships and slow progress in putting their lives back together and moving forward. Many callers had become entrepreneurs, using the experience of sudden job loss as an opportunity to strike out on their own.

It hadn't been easy for any of them. But their sense of accomplishment and positive attitude in recounting these challenges were evident; truly impressive! With enthusiasm, they spoke of their achievements, thankful for the crises which had challenged them to stretch and grow.

Most of these callers to Limbaugh's program were not only survivors, but had gone on to achieve even greater degrees of success and fulfillment. Faced with challenges, motivated people build their own mental bleachers, filling the stands with cheering thoughts that spur them on to win, no matter what.

Who Will Be Happier?

Reporter John Stossel explored the subject of happiness in an excellent TV special.

He interviewed a young man who had sustained serious injuries in an automobile collision, leaving him a quadriplegic. One year had passed.

The quadriplegic had faced his physical challenges with a positive spirit, using what most people would call a tragedy as an opportunity to change careers. He was now a teacher. His disability hadn't kept him from gaining a new sense of purpose in life. Satisfaction from helping others brought him even greater fulfillment.

Stossel's report concluded that genuine happiness is usually linked to having a worthwhile purpose.

Transforming Tragedy into Talent

Occasionally, I have exhibited at art shows with an exceptional artist named Eric. His story is also inspiring.

While driving home from the beach one summer afternoon in 1963, Eric was nearly killed when another car slammed into his Volkswagen Beetle. At 17, he suddenly found himself a quadriplegic.

Doctors told Eric he would never walk again. He refused to believe them. But, after a year with no improvement, the grim truth of his condition hit Eric hard. Reality crushed his spirit. He spent the next year filled with anger and bitterness. Friends eventually stopped visiting him.

Finally, Eric's mother gave him an ultimatum. "Either do something with your life...or go into a nursing home. You're not going to stay here and feel sorry for yourself." Her words were spoken out of tough love, and fortunately they reached Eric. He chose to turn his attitude around. He took positive action. Holding a paintbrush between his teeth, Eric developed dynamic desire, painstakingly training himself to be an artist.

It took many months of determined practice, but Eric's efforts eventually bore creative fruit. His artwork became good enough to sell. He perfected an artistic technique which he launched into a full-time, profitable business.

Eric became part of a cottage industry, employing a number of people to frame and market his fine work, as well as to manage the financial side of his business.

At the time of the collision, Eric's doctors predicted he'd live only 15 to 20 years. That was over 50 years ago. He continued working daily, spending 7½ hours in his wheelchair, paintbrush between his teeth, producing art, filling his life with purpose. Long ago, he chose to meet his personal challenges with grace and grit. Eric's dynamic desire brought forth an abiding skill he could share with thousands of others, and increased his longevity.

Thought Versus Feeling

A few people think things through; most only think they do. Not many people trudge up the stairs of thought. Most glide along on escalators of feeling. "I don't feel like doing that." Sounds familiar, doesn't it? For many, it becomes a non-motivating detriment in their lives, as they give in to being disciples of impulse.

It's far easier to follow your feelings than it is to command your thoughts. But it's best not to allow just your emotions to guide you. Follow your heart, but back up your feelings with sound judgment. Where feelings rule, rational thought is in exile. Think things through to create feelings that will serve you well.

On days when I don't feel like sitting at my easel to draw, and they are many, I park myself in front of it for several hours anyway. Some days are productive, others are not; but I'm there at the same time, daily. It's worth it.

The choice to override emotional impulse with mental diligence will eventually pay big dividends for you too.

Professional writers stress the importance of disciplined routine in their work. Empty sheets of paper, or a blank screen, can be daunting to a writer. But feelings of dread are shoved aside through discipline. The number of pages written daily may be zero or 20, good or bad. Nonetheless, the most disciplined writers write every day...until they reach their self-imposed deadline or word count goal.

Establish a productive routine for yourself and stay with it. Impulsive feelings will always float through the ballroom of your mind, but you don't have to dance with them.

Make every decision in the house of reason. Keep emotion outside, even when it presses its nose against the window and begs to come in. Remain with the rhythm of your productive routine. It's generally not smart to take action solely based on your feelings. Hold feelings as "a call to thought." Think before you act.

Prune Your Dead Branches

In our backyard stands a century-old maple tree we call the Grand Old Lady. Dead branches were carefully trimmed away some years ago to improve her health and form.

In summer, the maple is lush with foliage, and our Grand Old Lady greets the autumn dressed in brilliant yellow-gold. Even the winter months find her looking majestic, strong winds having little effect on her sturdy branches. Pruning has strengthened and enhanced this lovely old tree.

How much dead wood do people carry around? Useless branches can often be seen everywhere. Debilitating and unattractive, they need to be cut from our lives. Rid yourself of any branches of self-doubt, laziness, procrastination, fear, discouragement, guilt, negativity, regret, ignorance, blame, resentment, irresponsibility, worry, rationalization, and any pretense or arrogance you may have.

Trimming away these and other dead branches strengthens, propels, and directs your energies in positive, healthy ways. Pruning is a powerful and necessary tool for personal growth. It fosters the development of your dynamic desire in working toward your potential.

Slow Down, Simplify and...*See*

By slowing down we can hasten our education. For example, Amish children cannot join the church until they become young adults, usually between the ages of 18 and 22. Prior to that, they often manage to get a taste of the outside world. Occasionally, rock music is heard blaring inside a horse-drawn buggy. Adolescent boys have been known to visit pool halls, drive cars, and sample alcoholic beverages. Despite these and other worldly temptations, 80 percent of Amish youth go on to join the church and choose to stay within the community.

Visitors to our inn and cottage are sometimes surprised to hear this. "That's a high percentage," a guest might say. "You'd think it would be hard for Amish kids to give up everything the modern world has to offer."

The Amish are basically a wise people, having boiled life down to its essentials. The quiet, uncluttered lifestyle they practice keeps them and their community in constant touch with Nature, in tune with the deeper, natural versus man-made world, resulting in more healthy rhythms for their daily lives. "Simplified but intense" might be a good way to describe the Amish culture.

All of us could benefit from this approach to living. You needn't sell your car, buy a horse, and grow a beard. You don't have to alter your attire or mode of transportation; just change your pace so that you're more clearly aware of what's really going on in your life.

In the rush to make ends meet and keep up with life's activities, we may be quick to lose sight of ourselves and our purpose or calling. Learn to slow down and practice a silent observation of your world. Insight comes when we quiet our minds. It is inner vision. It is learning to see and understand on a more profound, expansive level.

Emily Dickinson was one of the country's greatest poets. She seldom left her home in Amherst, Massachusetts. Within the uncomplicated world of that house and an outside garden, she discovered the special quality which life holds even in its simplest forms.

Emily Dickinson's intense power of observation was transformed into hundreds of short poems, created in easy words, but containing profound meaning. The poet narrowed the parameters of her physical world, broadened her inner vision, and saw life more clearly.

Listen intently amid the world's noise, and you'll always hear music. Stop and smell the roses.

My innkeeper-wife is an artist in our kitchen. She loves to cook. I watch her create delicious broths and sauces by reducing them over high heat…boiling the liquids down to half their original volume. This greatly intensifies the flavor of what remains in the pot.

In the noisy chaos of daily life (for most of us, anyway), we need to engage in our own form of reduction. We can do this by rising early each morning to spend some time in silent solitude. Treasure these moments; use them for reading an empowering book or planning your day so you can incorporate working toward accomplishing your desire.

Hauling yourself out of a nice warm bed earlier than you're used to is a ritual that requires tenacity. You may be resistant to the idea in the beginning. I understand those feelings. I've had them myself. But this disciplined action, arduous at first, will soon open your mind to fresh perspectives and insights. You'll carry them with you the rest of your day and on into the rest of your life. As they guide you to discern what is essential and good, your life will intensify in joyful discovery.

Time with Yourself Sets the Stage for Your Day

Though I'm going to repeat myself, it's not a sign of early senility. The last two paragraphs need emphasis. A stronger, more creative and productive you cannot be formed in the thick of the daily routine. The frenzied swirl of others' demands, expectations, and negative opinions makes that virtually impossible.

Step out of the world and into your life. Stake your claim to 60 minutes of daily, personal, goal-oriented time, and defend it against all intrusions. This time with yourself is essential for living deeply in the world without being consumed by it.

Rub the sleep from your eyes tomorrow morning and awaken to new possibilities. In time, you'll become well-acquainted with your vast potential for achieving your desire. An inner peaceful calm awaits you, designed to keep you in mental balance between your need for personal growth and life's demands on your time and energy.

Would you like to follow, as Henry David Thoreau would say, "The beat of a different drummer"? How about beating your own drum instead? This is what ritual solitude can help you do. Distance yourself from the world early every morning and focus on developing your gift of desire.

Process and the Goal

Most diets fail, even when people succeed in taking off excess weight. During weeks or months of sacrifice and denial, dieters long for the day when they'll be thin again and able to eat, in moderation, all the foods they enjoy.

Unfortunately, their moderation approach seldom works in the long-term, as they haven't changed their unhealthy thinking and habits. They most likely haven't resolved the underlying issues they may blame or not even realize are causing them to overeat and fail to get and stay active. So the surplus poundage slowly, sometimes quickly, returns or increases as their frustrations mount.

The key to losing weight and keeping it off is to abandon the idea of short-term, quick-fix, yo-yo dieting altogether. Sustained weight loss requires altering the way in which we view food. Any temporary change in our eating and activity behaviors, from drastic to mild, to reach some ideal goal, will ultimately fail. The healthy food choices you make and the portions you need to eat in order to maintain an ideal weight, coupled with the physical activity you engage in, needs to become a permanent part of your daily life.

"In my world there is no such thing as a potato," said comedian Sid Caesar. A beefy man during his TV heyday in the 1950s, Caesar managed to stay thin for four decades. He and other successful healthy eaters and exercisers focus on the process and the goal.

First they decide where they want to be weight-wise. Then they devise or follow an eating and exercise plan to lose the excess weight and maintain their new weight for the rest of their lives. These people approach weight loss with the understanding that modest, permanent changes are much preferred to severe, short-term ones.

This dedication to goal and process is applicable to any passionate endeavor. It's important to focus on a desired outcome or you'll be aimless in your pursuit—*a wandering generality!* Follow your dream, whatever it is, while finding pleasure in your daily actions by working creatively, and loving what you do. Then you can know fulfillment all along the way to your goal. Joy in the process of doing brings satisfaction and bolsters you during moments of failure, which are valuable learning experiences in the pursuit of your dream.

Resilience comes to those who keep their eyes on the goal and dedicate themselves to the doing. Our real joy in life needs to be discovered during those long stretches of time between moments of achievement. The journey is the success—a *continuing* realization of worthwhile dreams, goals, and objectives, which are determined by your purpose for being here, your calling; how you can best make a difference.

Some Facts About the Rich

One of my pet peeves is the mistaken belief that the ability to succeed is determined by how much money someone has. We may look at affluent people and think they had an easier time of it, or an unfair advantage. There's a lot of class envy in society, all misguided.

Here are some facts about the rich among us, culled from Thomas J. Stanley's eye-opening book, *The Millionaire Next Door*. Eighty percent of millionaires in America are first-generation wealthy. Nothing was given to them—they earned it. To look at these people, you'd never know they were rich.

Many of the wealthy among us actually live in middle-class neighborhoods. Usually married only once, they are frugal and great savers. They hold traditional values. Who are they? The majority are dry cleaners, bowling alley owners, scrap metal haulers, and small business owners—not doctors or lawyers or born wealthy.

Most millionaires have a strong belief in themselves and a dedication to their dreams. They accumulated their wealth slowly and steadily, with patient perseverance. Money didn't just fall into their laps. Discard the myth that most wealthy people are evil exploiters of the working people. They *are* hard working, dedicated people who also are persistent and work smart. When they achieve financial well-being and freedom they usually continue working because they enjoy being productive members of society...and making a difference.

Know these facts and you'll understand what separates the rich from the average. It's not class or money; it's determination, discipline, and action. These people continuously develop their dynamic desire so they can live their dreams. Recognizing this is the first step toward becoming one of them.

You don't need money to be successful—you need to be successful to have money! It's the result of consistently blasting through and learning from failures, driven by your desire.

Don't Let Gossip Distract You

People love to gossip. In offices, places of worship, and neighborhoods, gossip is a shortcut many take in a vain attempt to feel good about themselves.

It's impossible to gain genuine self-improvement when we sit back and gleefully tear down the people around us. Gossip is so convenient. It's a tempting, titillating, easy habit to slip into. Chattering about the faults and flawed behaviors of others puffs us up with a feeling of superiority. But what does it accomplish? What success does it lead to? None!

Not only is gossip not helpful, it's both hurtful and devious. It corrodes our character. The false sense of superiority gossip gives masks our own personal shortcomings and distracts us from the disciplined work we need to be doing to better ourselves and our lives.

Growing up, I remember my dad reciting these words from Robert Louis Stevenson: "There is so much good in the worst of us, and so much bad in the best of us, that it behooves all of us not to talk about the rest of us." Gossiping is a poor use of valuable time. Instead of talking about others, become someone others will rave about and emulate.

Think of friends, relatives, and coworkers you know who like to gossip. They spend so much time each day finding fault instead of looking for the good in people around them. Why do they do that? What is it about some people that compels them to tear others down?

I'm no Rhodes Scholar, but I do know that people who genuinely like themselves, those who have a passion for excellence and keep a positive attitude, don't feel the need to gossip. They don't look for flaws in others in order to feel better about themselves. Negativity gets you nowhere.

Associate only with positive-thinking people who live each day in quiet self-confidence and always have a kind word for others. Such people are following their dreams and making a difference in the world.

Preparation and Patience

If success were a freshly painted old house, some people would stand across the street from it and say, "Sure, that house looks great. It's easy when you have the right brushes, a ladder, and enough paint to get the job done."

What goes unappreciated by these admirers is the tedious preparation necessary for the painting to be done; many hours of careful scraping, sanding, and patching were spent to ensure that the project would be beautifully completed. The wood also had to be primed before the finish coats were applied. To bypass this work and just slap on a coat or two would soon result in a house with its paint cracked, blistered, and peeling away from the wood.

When we stand across the street from success, it's fine to be dazzled by the attractive results, but we also need to appreciate the time involved in doing the job properly. Keep in mind the patient preparation required to achieve any worthwhile goal.

Some of us may like to fantasize that our life should be like a movie. We may envision ourselves becoming a success, conveniently suffering and overcoming all the frustrations and awkward stumblings of a lifetime within a neat two-hour period.

How romantic and exciting the pursuit of a goal would be if we could just condense and tighten our experiences. Wouldn't it be nice to live only those events which propel us forward to fulfill our dream in just one sitting? Why not throw in some popcorn while you're at it?

When success doesn't come easily, people often don't want to continue making the effort...and quit on themselves. That's why most people live average, routine lives; they don't want to bother with anything beyond the grind they're in. They don't like what they're doing, yet refuse to change.

Face it, there are often many obstacles to overcome in the process of getting where we truly long to be. But challenges in the pursuit of what we love—our dream—are bearable. They're just part of the necessary process. Our desire, when dynamic enough, will help to sustain us.

My grandmother liked to say, "Honey, put one foot in front of the other and keep moving forward." Widowed at 50, she was left to fend for herself at a time when women were largely dependent upon their husbands for economic survival.

Grandma Horner, a woman of great determination, slowly acquired the skills of an astute businesswoman. She involved herself in the community, joining a variety of charitable organizations. Her perseverance through painful loss strengthened her self-confidence and enriched her life.

Long-term success cannot be like a snapshot, achieved with the clicking of a shutter. Such success is a jigsaw-puzzle photograph, created bit by bit, with patience and persistence, until all the pieces are in place.

Don't demand perfection from yourself. Locate perfection on the map, then set out on foot to get there, visiting as many educational sites as possible along the way. But don't ever expect to arrive at perfection. Instead, strive for excellence. Develop patience. It usually takes a long time to become really accomplished. Long-term success requires long-term commitment.

My first drawings looked terrible. Slowly, over a period of several years, I began to see improvement. Fortunately, I understood early on that you don't need to be good at it to be an artist; you just need to *want* to be good at it and keep consistently working at it.

Don't expect to be an instant success. Give yourself time to grow and succeed. Nurture your dream. Again, don't compare yourself to others more accomplished than you are. That wouldn't be fair to you. Your task is to focus on your own progress, comparing yourself today with how you were yesterday. Have you improved?

Creating a detailed drawing teaches patience. Some of my pieces take more than 300 hours to complete. You learn, as an artist, to think incrementally. To sit in front of a blank sheet of paper and envision a completed drawing can be quite intimidating, so I never do that. My goal, a finished work of art, is broken down into many smaller goals, painstaking steps made slowly with determination that eventually take me to where I want to be.

For writers, it isn't a book or an article they write, it's one word at a time. For composers, it's one note, then another, and another. Creativity isn't a product. It's an incremental process, a way of doing things. Be sure to set incremental goals, but not so high that you dislocate a shoulder in your stretch to reach them.

It's always easier for us just to think of the future than it is to act in the present to create the future we really want. Many are in love with the idea of being artists, writers, composers, actors, business owners, and such.

Many romanticize and fantasize about what it must be like, but they never get around to the practicality of actually doing and experiencing. Whatever you want to do well will most likely require much practice and learning. Leave your frustration at the door and find joy in the process. Don't take yourself too seriously—have fun with it!

A Big Task Broken Down into Small Increments Is Doable

Jane Taylor, a British writer of juvenile fiction in the early 19th Century, told a fable about an old kitchen clock with a pendulum that suddenly decided to stop moving.

"I'm tired of ticking," the pendulum tells the clock's face. "This morning, I calculated how many times I'd have to tick in the course of only the next 24 hours."

The thought of ticking 86,400 times a day had exhausted it, so the pendulum quit. Multiplying those strokes by the number of weeks and months in a year only increased the pendulum's discouragement.

The clock's face listened to the pendulum's complaint, then calmly asked him to tick just six more times. After the pendulum did so, the face asked, "Was that at all fatiguing?"

"Not in the least," said the pendulum. "It's not of six strokes that I complain, nor of sixty, but of millions."

The face tells the pendulum to keep in mind that, although it can think of a million strokes in an instant, it only needs to tick once in any given moment. It just needs to focus on "the present moment in which it needs to swing."

Viewed in this way, the pendulum delightfully sees its task as no longer overwhelming, so it resumes ticking as loud as ever.

Cultivate Restless Patience

Necessity may be the mother of Invention, but its father is always Restlessness. Cultivate a restless patience. Carefully structure each day, devoting time daily toward the achievement of your dream. In this way you build a small fire within yourself. You become eager for accomplishment.

Accept that, in moving forward, you'll be taking one step at a time. This can be challenging but you can do it. On some days your pace will be brisk, maybe breaking into a run, while on other days, you may only take a measured step or two.

At times you'll find yourself standing still, in need of encouragement, which is only natural. Remain focused and disciplined, knowing that doubt and frustration are everpresent, ready to thwart your efforts. But you can overcome these foes of success by your faith and determination.

Wanting to leapfrog over obstacles and get to where you want to be is normal, but you need to temper restlessness with patience. Concentrate on maintaining forward momentum. Balance the full scope of your journey, keeping the big picture in mind, with an acceptance that many individual steps are required on the path you've chosen.

Live in each step with a self-engendered enthusiasm. It's an inside job. Walk, sprint, tumble, leap, or crawl—but remain steadily on that path. Fill yourself with restless patience. A continual moving forward by inches will put you miles ahead of most people because they are stuck in a rut rather than on track to their dreams.

Be flexible. Remain solid of purpose, but keep fluid the means to achieve it. To fulfill a dream, it isn't enough to just push forward. Know when to jump back, skip sideways, or pause to do an occasional headstand on your path. When pushing forward, don't just push hard. Push thoughtfully.

Passion with Patient Perseverance Creates Talent

"This carpet has got to go," said my wife, shortly after moving into our home. The wall-to-wall carpeting throughout our house, originally harvest gold, was later dyed an apple green. Now, after 20 years, its blonde roots were again showing through in spots.

We decided to tear out all the carpeting out, hoping to restore our home's original 1853 floors. That would depend, of course, on the condition of the wood.

Careful chiseling and prying away of the sub-flooring exposed random-width planks of pine and fir. They looked to be in pretty good shape. Since I did a poor impression of Bob Vila, then-host of the popular TV show *This Old House,* we hired professionals to sand and finish the floors.

Jeff and Carey Hoover are brothers whose reputation for fine restoration work is well-known in our area. Jeff, the older one, gave us a good history lesson about our floors, telling us, "The wood used here came from trees more than a century old when they were cut down 150 years ago. The logs were first floated in the river, or else put into a holding pool of cold water. That forced the sap deep into the wood."

"Why was that done?" I asked.

"Think of it as an early form of pressure-treating," Jeff said. "It preserved the wood. When we sand your floors today, 150 years later, we can still smell sap!"

Jeff has great respect for the quality of materials used in the past. "We'll go to some of these old farmhouses and find bare windowsills. No paint on them for thirty years or more. We just sand a little, and then prime and paint; and the sills are as good as new. You couldn't do that with today's wood."

"Why not?" I asked.

"Mature trees, the kind used to build your home, were slow growing. That makes for sturdy wood. After so many years, the tree's rings are very close together. The wood is dense, and more durable."

Jeff thinks people move too fast today. "Time is our enemy now," he told me. "Technology wows us with its speed, but we lose so much in the process. Trees are force-grown and harvested quickly. They're cut younger, so the rings are spread out. The wood lacks density.

"Latent sap gives wood its long life, but logs are no longer put into cold water. Now they're kiln-dried. Today's wood has no life to it. It begins to rot from the inside, even on expensive new houses." Jeff shook his head sadly. "We've sacrificed quality for speed," he said.

Jeff's observations about the quality of wood also apply to the quality of people's lives. Most of us, to some degree, sacrifice quality for speed. Ours is a society where too many expect the instant gratification of their desires. What they want, they want *now*.

But things of substance and value take time to develop. Excellence can't be rushed into being just by the strength of desire. Passion without patience has no real life to it, and many goals soon rot from the inside. Discipline yourself to work and wait. Passion and patient perseverance aren't substitutes for talent—they're the parents from which talents are spawned.

Slow your mind to a realistic speed while you're in pursuit of any meaningful endeavor. Time becomes your most valuable partner once you learn to work at its methodical pace. Patience, persistence, and wholehearted dedication hold a quiet power.

Gigantic inflexible aspirations, not broken down into reasonable chunks, seldom rise very high. Ambitions built slowly, brick by brick, goal by goal, are best. "Great things are not done by impulse," wrote Vincent van Gogh, "but by a series of small things brought together."

Blunders, Bungles, and Boners—*Oh My!*

We're always going to make mistakes. Accept it as a part of being human and keep going. Weather forecasters do it with ease. They tell us to "expect a sunny day tomorrow," and we wake up to rain. They warn that "a blizzard is on the way," and "everyone" hurries to the supermarket for bread and milk. But not a flake falls.

How do weather people react to these inaccuracies? They smile, shrug their shoulders, and proceed to give you the best five-day forecast they can. They don't expect to always be right. We enjoy poking fun at them with comments like, "In what other profession could you be so consistently wrong and still keep your job?"

The truth is that weather forecasters are usually correct. It's just easy for us to target them for their mistakes. We do the same thing to ourselves. We dwell on personal blunders, bungles, and boners, beating ourselves up over errors in judgment, as if progress were possible without them! This self-torture often inhibits us from going forward.

Let's take a lesson from weather forecasters. We need to realize that outside forces and our own mistakes may trip us up occasionally. Goof-ups may make us look silly, but what is sillier is our unwillingness to smile, shrug our shoulders, and move forward with confidence.

Gifts Are the Result of Diligent Work—*Not Birth*

John is a successful nature photographer. Admirers of his wildlife studies and majestic landscapes sometimes ask him, "Is this a gift, or are you self-taught?"

"This is a gift I got for Christmas one year," he tells them, his eyes twinkling. After taking a moment to enjoy their puzzled reaction, he explains the creative process. "First, I develop the idea for a photograph, then mentally picture the scene I want to capture. Then I pack up and go to that part of the country where I'm most likely to get it."

Some people think beautiful wildlife photography is the result of sitting quietly in the woods, waiting for something to happen. "I wish it were that easy," says John. "I single out an animal and study it, learning its habits and routine. Then I work to make the photographic image I have in mind happen, a process of ten days or more, and even then I don't always get the shot I want."

John is a good-natured, patient man, with dogged determination. "If I quit at that point, I'd be a failure as a nature photographer," he says. "I keep going back to the same area, sometimes many trips over a period of two or three years, until I come home with the photograph I want."

In addition to a fine eye and good sense of composition, John has a strong background in animal research and broad geographical knowledge. Through years of painstaking study and travel, he knows every part of the US, and its animals.

"I've been chased by all kinds of critters," John told me. He has shinnied up countless trees to avoid angry bull elk, was knocked down by a grizzly, and routinely faces threats from a host of other animals. It requires far more than the clicking of a shutter to capture John's beautiful photographs. It takes decades of determined preparation, practice, and perseverance. Excellence always takes time.

With *Dynamic* Desire, Success Can Be Achieved *Under All Kinds of Circumstances*

If you fail to reach a goal, it doesn't mean you're a failure. You simply learned something that doesn't work. So you need to take a different approach.

Franklin Delano Roosevelt was stricken with polio at age 39 and lost the use of his legs. His goal was to walk again. He was determined to find some procedure, therapy, or exercise that would produce a cure. But he never did.

I guess you could say that, in one sense, FDR failed. He didn't get the result he was looking for in that area of his life. But look at the bigger picture. His boundless enthusiasm and determination didn't give him back his legs. Instead, they gave him the presidency of the United States.

His positive spirit and tenacity stirred a nation that was in the depths of the Depression. He gave people hope when they desperately needed it. You needn't agree with FDR's politics to appreciate his undying optimism. He had the right attitude and approach to guide a nation through the Depression and World War II.

I wonder if Roosevelt would have become president had he not lost the use of his legs. That challenge brought out the best in him. His courageous spirit served him well, taking him to the pinnacle of political achievement.

For every failed effort you point to, I can show you others who faced greater obstacles, tougher circumstances, and more devastating setbacks, yet they still managed to overcome them all to achieve their desires.

There's great danger in believing that some are destined to fail, no matter what they do. When the going gets tough and the frustration level grows, you may also believe you're one of those for whom failure is just inevitable. But that losing attitude would be a self-fulfilling prophecy. Refuse to accept failure as a final condition in life. In your effort to succeed, you, like FDR, might not get exactly what you want, but you may get more than you ever dreamed possible.

Stop Trying...*Start Doing!*
We're more likely to succeed in life if we never try to reach a goal.

How's that again?

We can't *try* to do anything. "Your own resolution to succeed," Lincoln said, "is more important than any other one thing." To be resolved is to be committed. We'll either do something, however long or how much effort it may take, or we won't. When we "try" to accomplish a goal, what we're implicitly saying is, "Well, I may not reach this goal, despite my efforts." Try is weak, often an excuse for not giving your all.

Listen to cigarette smokers who say, "I've tried to quit." But what does that really mean? They stopped smoking until their discomfort level grew too high, at which point they returned to the habit. When you've truly resolved to quit smoking and nicotine withdrawal begins, you don't light up. You persevere through the pain because you're committed to your decision to stop smoking. As soon as you do that, you've joined the ranks of the non-smokers.

The same is true for overeaters and alcoholics, and anyone else who chooses to make a positive, permanent change in life. It's challenging, and takes total commitment. If you say, "I'll try," you give yourself an out. Erase "try" from your vocabulary and substitute with the words, "I'm doing it!"

Be a Darned Fool—*You'll Love the Results*

Comedian W.C. Fields jokingly said, "If at first you don't succeed, try, try again, then quit. No sense being a darned fool about it." Fields obviously never applied this only-for-laughs advice to his own life. As a young boy, he longed to become a great juggler, so he practiced tirelessly, obsessed with the desire to juggle. At times, he could be found crying in frustration, but he simply wouldn't quit. He remained a darned fool about it. He wasn't a born juggler, but he had dynamic desire. He did it wrong until he got it right.

Fields learned to juggle, juggling his way into vaudeville, performing in the world's top theaters. Later, he juggled his way into the movies, making comedy history, and took the secrets of his juggling routines to his grave that have never been duplicated.

Whatever you desire to do, be a darned fool about it, and never let failure get you down. Mickey Rooney said, "You always pass failure on the way to success." He knew from experience. His life was a roller coaster of ups and downs, but, through it all, he persevered with dynamic desire.

"Never confuse a single defeat with a final defeat." That's great advice from writer F. Scott Fitzgerald.

You can either sink in the mud of frustration or slog through it and get to the other side. People who win are, in reality, soldiers-to-be in boot camp. But picture them marching in a parade with music playing, banners flying, and medals glimmering on their chests.

Successful people have fallen more often than the rest of humanity. They've just refused to *stay* down. They continue to pick themselves up, always doing their best to follow their dreams and make a difference.

Sightless, Soundless Vision—*A "Gift" Beyond Compare*

"We can do anything we want to do if we stick to it long enough." Do you know who said that? Helen Keller. As a young girl, she faced obstacles to success almost too horrendous to contemplate. How do you learn to speak, read, or reason, when your eyes can't see and your ears can't hear? How do you begin to communicate with the outside world when your inner world is silent darkness?

Thanks to Annie Sullivan, a wonderful teacher and friend, Helen Keller came to understand that, despite her severe physical limitations, she, too, possessed abundant potential. She grew to become an inspirational example of successful living for people throughout the world. The woman literally walked with kings. "Life is either a daring adventure," she wrote, "or nothing at all."

If Helen Keller could accomplish this with no functional eyes or ears, imagine what you could do with *your* life! Next time you feel like the odds are against you, think of Helen Keller. Don't make excuses. Use disabilities, disadvantages, and challenges as catalysts to propel you in excelling, doubling down in developing your dynamic desire.

Perfect Circles

It's impossible to draw a perfect circle, right? Let me tell you about my eighth-grade science teacher. It was his first year of teaching, and I remember he talked a lot about the planets, drawing them as circles on the blackboard. From September to June, he drew his planets so many times that, by the end of the school year, he was drawing nearly flawless circles. Do anything long enough and you can get good at it!

The Freedom to Be Great—*By Emulating the Great*

You can go wherever you choose in life, but only you can get yourself there. That doesn't mean you have to go it alone. The wisest consultants in the world, living or not, continue to serve us and are reached by reading books. Study their lives. Absorb the richness of knowledge and insight they have to offer. Ask your mentor or leader to recommend some books to you.

One of my favorite "consultants" is Frederick Douglass. He was born a slave in 19th Century America. As a boy, Douglass knew he possessed the potential for greatness, born in every human being. Imagine how trapped he must have felt, denied the freedom to realize his potential.

Well, the slave owner's wife showed compassion for young Frederick and began teaching him how to read. When her husband discovered what she was doing, he quickly put an end to it. But by then it was too late. Learning to read had become an obsession with Douglass. Even at his young age, he knew that education and dedicated work would be his ticket to freedom and success.

133

He managed to get his hands on a book of great world speeches. Douglass not only learned how to read that book, he absorbed its contents and committed it to memory. That's how hungry he was to better himself. Just think: Memorize the world's greatest speeches and you can also learn how to organize your thoughts, how to reason, and how to persuade others.

Douglass kept his growing knowledge hidden, biding his time until he could make his escape to freedom. He endured the indignities and occasional lashings—the unfair treatment given him by ignorant men. Eventually, he did escape to the North, becoming the most eloquent spokesman for the black cause in 19th Century America. President Lincoln would refer to him as "my friend, Douglass."

Now, if Frederick Douglass could rise above such bleak circumstances to fulfill his dreams, what excuse could we possibly have for not succeeding in life? *Excuses are self-injected embalming fluid.*

Both Frederick Douglass and Helen Keller were created from the same materials used to make you and me. Their gift was their desire, which they dynamically developed, enabling them to succeed. That's a choice available to everyone.

Enlist for the long haul when you honestly want to earn the rank of "Successful."

Fat Man with a Lisp—*Dynamic Desire Turned His Challenge into a Gift*

"Never give in, never. Never, never. Never...."

When his facial features were compared with those of a bulldog, Winston Churchill was pleased. He noted that the bulldog's nose was short and slanted backward. In this way, he said, the dog could continue to breathe without letting go of his prey.

Like a bulldog on a mailman, Churchill never let go. His tenacity made him one of the most beloved and important figures of the 20th Century. Without that bulldog trait, he would have never made it into the history books.

In childhood, Churchill was lonely and shy. His parents were preoccupied with their busy social lives and virtually ignored him. Raised by a nanny and sent away to school at age seven, Churchill began exhibiting bulldog tendencies in his teens. Suffering from a pronounced stutter and lisp, he dealt with both by joining a debate society, where he soon overcame these challenges and flourished.

As a young man he served in the military, published books, and later was elected to the British Parliament. By the late 1920s, however, his political career appeared to be over. Voted out in 1929, at 55, he was seen as washed-up, over the hill. Churchill spent the 1930s nearly forgotten. But he focused on his career as an author, and never stopped writing.

For almost a decade he warned Britain and the world about Adolph Hitler. With great foresight, he described what would happen if Europe failed to prepare an adequate military defense. No one listened to him. He was viewed as an old man whose relevance had seemingly passed.

Like a bulldog, Churchill kept breathing and wouldn't let go. He continued to make accurate predictions about Germany's expansionist plans and, when Hitler's troops began to march across Europe, his call to re-arm was remembered. At 66 the British elected him Prime Minister, and the supposedly washed-up old man was suddenly an inspirational leader who rallied his people, guiding them through their darkest days.

As Churchill said, "Never give in, never. Never, never. Never…." Inspiration dawns only on those who stay awake to prepare for its arrival.

Success can be created out of any failure provided you learn from it and keep moving ahead. If you don't fall apart when your plans do, a large measure of success is already yours. Each failure is another step forward. Defeat conquers only those who sit down and give up the quest. So long as your heart keeps beating and you keep going, you'll experience no real dead ends in life.

Four Stories of Uncommon Discipline, Perseverance, and Dynamic Desire

Winners at slot machines strongly influence the people around them. You stand at a slot, feeding it quarters and pulling the lever, just to have your change disappear. Meanwhile, the guy to your left keeps hitting winning combinations. Bells are ringing. Quarters gush from his machine.

You glance to your right, just in time to see a woman win the jackpot. She's jumping up and down. Your slot-machine neighbors don't look any smarter than you, but *they're* winning! So you continue to drop quarters, five at a time now, into your machine. The infectious effect of seeing others hit the jackpot spurs you on to also become a winner.

In casinos, it's only the management which ultimately becomes successful. But the psychological principle at work there can be used to make you a *real* winner in life. When we acquaint ourselves with those who overcame seemingly insurmountable obstacles to achieve their dreams, as in the following four examples, their stories can inspire and help us develop our own dynamic desire to succeed.

Nice Girls Didn't—*But She Had Dynamic Desire*

At 25, Florence Nightingale decided to dedicate her life to a career in nursing, horrifying her parents. As affluent people they thought it was disgraceful that she would choose such a lowly profession. In 1845 hospitals were crowded, unsanitary places. Their stench nauseated visitors. Nurses were often drunk and of low character, sometimes supplementing their meager income by turning to prostitution.

In short, "Nice girls didn't." Eight years would pass before Florence could openly pursue her dream. She was more than a little depressed when she said, "No advantage that I can see comes of my living on. I shall never do anything and am worse than dust and nothing.... Oh, for some strong thing to sweep this loathsome life into the past."

Florence remained ever the dutiful daughter at home with her parents. But the fire of dynamic desire was within her, and not even depression could put it out. She rose each morning before dawn to study, by candlelight, reports of the unsanitary conditions in the London, Paris, and Berlin hospitals. She filled notebooks with statistical information about the deplorable state of public health, keeping detailed records of all that she learned.

A 26-year-old Florence wrote, "I feel as if all my being were gradually drawing together to one point." She was focused, committed! But every attempt to apply her growing knowledge was thwarted by family pressure to act in accordance with their high station in life. So, while Florence remained at home, she continued her studies in secret.

Over the next several years her torment and sense of worthlessness increased, at times driving her to the verge of madness. She felt that she'd accomplished nothing in life. "Busy idleness" was how she described her life condition.

At 31, Florence finally managed to break away from her family to take medical training, first at a German institute with religious roots, then in a Paris hospital where the nurses were nuns. She finally took a nursing position in a London hospital. Her desire to nurse was, to her mind, a calling to serve—it was her mission.

Hospital positions at that time were often secured either through bribery or nepotism. A nurse's qualifications were seldom the primary factor considered at hiring time. Florence fought the system. She became a one-woman crusade for better quality nurses and doctors. A skillful negotiator, she made many important contacts among people of prominence, enlisting their support to bring about reforms in the hospital where she worked.

Out of consideration for those of you who have eaten within the past 24 hours, I won't detail the squalid conditions of European hospital wards in the mid-19th Century. Let this example suffice: During the Crimean War, hospitals swelled with the wounded. Imagine a thousand soldiers suffering from diarrhea in a hospital equipped with only 20 chamber pots.

Florence Nightingale served the cause in a Constantinople military hospital, where she faced a seemingly insurmountable task. She had to improve sanitary conditions, train a qualified staff of nurses and doctors, and overcome political corruption and petty jealousies. Accustomed to comfort and luxury, this determined woman lived under the worst conditions imaginable, but she was on a mission. "Resignation…," she wrote, "I never understood that word."

The hospitalized soldiers adored her. As a show of respect, they even gave up swearing! Those who recuperated and later returned home to their families spoke of her kindness to them. Stories of her sacrifice and caring spread throughout England. Florence Nightingale became a national heroine. Queen Victoria, herself, came to praise her efforts.

During this time, Florence also improved the wounded soldiers' intellectual and spiritual lives, encouraging the men to send money home, better themselves, and give up drinking. She further assisted them to reform their personal behavior by helping to open schools for the soldiers' education. Florence accomplished all of this while suffering a variety of personal health challenges. A slight woman who never enjoyed good health, she endured sciatic pain, recurring earaches, laryngitis, and chronic bouts of insomnia. Despite these physical ailments, she managed, in just a few years, to revolutionize how the public viewed nurses, doctors, and British soldiers.

Seventy-three percent of the deaths during the Crimean War were due to disease. At home after the war, Florence paced her room at night, driven to formulate a plan for the complete overhaul of the Army Medical Department. Once genuine reform of military hospitals was underway, she turned her attention to improving conditions in civil hospitals as well.

Dealing with the inflated egos of bureaucrats was a constant source of frustration, and it took its toll on her health. At one point, she became so ill that the *London Daily News* wrote her obituary in expectation of her imminent demise.

Florence rallied. By age 39, she was an invalid who seldom left her bedroom, and never left the house. Yet she continued to work relentlessly for reform in every aspect of patient care, medical training, and hospital design—even suggesting the most soothing color to paint hospital room walls. She opened a school for aspiring nurses, training them to her own high standards. Next came a school for the training of midwives.

Only 40 years old, she required constant physical care. "I am so much weaker," she wrote, "that I do not sit up at all now." But she wouldn't let her health challenges impede her progress or lessen her administrative efforts. Through reams of correspondence during the US Civil War, she guided the War Department with her detailed instructions for hospital reorganization and improved patient care. Later, she became a pioneer of the first Red Cross movement.

Florence Nightingale could have been the poster girl for the keys to success. Her faith, commitment to purpose, and inexhaustible energy to act on her dreams were astounding testimonials to the power of developing dynamic desire. "I think one's feelings waste themselves in words," she said. "They ought all to be distilled into actions which bring results."

Tenacity in Developing Dynamic Desire Reveals the Gift

"Blessed is he who carries within himself a God, an ideal, and who obeys it," said scientist Louis Pasteur. "[An] ideal of art, ideal of science, ideal of the gospel virtues, therein lie the springs of great thoughts and actions; they all reflect light from the Infinite." Louis Pasteur's own life exemplified the truth of these words.

In his teens he displayed a strong analytical ability. His mind worked so painstakingly on problems that some teachers thought he was slow. Naturally inquisitive, he immersed himself in his studies. Leisure time was spent at the library, where he enjoyed reading biographies of great men and women. He was hungry to learn and benefit from the experiences of illustrious people.

Pasteur's powers of examination and investigation eventually led him into the field of chemistry. At the time he lived, in the mid-19th Century, scientists saw a great many people fall sick and die from disease. He was determined to understand the workings of microorganisms, and to find ways to prevent the spread of germs.

Pasteur held the "wild theory" that germs were spread by floating through the air, contaminating food and drink, causing people to contract a wide variety of deadly diseases. His ideas were considered scientific heresy by many of his peers.

The widely accepted belief then was that germs were caused by spontaneous generation; that they somehow arose from inanimate matter, and scientists were at a loss as to how to stop the process. Pasteur endured much criticism and personal attack from the scientific establishment, who felt their scientific reputations were threatened by his opinions.

Surgical operations in his day were often successful, but patients died anyway. Doctors didn't understand the need to sterilize against germs. No one took precautions that are now routine. Creating an antiseptic environment for patients wasn't even a consideration.

Louis Pasteur's research was instrumental in changing that. He demonstrated the need for sterilization against germs to protect people on the operating table from infectious diseases. He also pioneered work in the creation of vaccines, giving patients a weakened strain of the germ to stimulate immunity to the disease.

At 42, he discovered that heating beer and wine killed most of the bacteria that cause spoilage, preventing them from turning sour. This led to his inventing pasteurization, which is used in the dairy and food industries for microbial control and food preservation.

During years of working in conflict with a hostile scientific community, Pasteur dealt with tremendous personal hardship. He buried three of his young children and, at 45, he suffered a debilitating stroke which paralyzed his entire left side.

The scientist turned to a hope-inducing habit from his youth. He read accounts of famous people who, through their courage and perseverance, overcame failure, illness, and other personal setbacks. Through long months of convalescence, Pasteur focused his mind on returning to work.

"A man's life is useless if not spent in service to others," he said. Three months after the stroke, he was carried back into his laboratory where, from his bed or sofa, he directed his assistants in research and scientific experiments.

Pasteur's dedication to his dream revolutionized the scientific community. His research saved countless lives from being lost to rabies, diphtheria, tuberculosis, and many other diseases. Toward the end of his life, he helped to create the Pasteur Institute, in Paris, where his important work to relieve human suffering could continue.

"Let me tell you the secret that has led me to my goal," Pasteur said. "My strength lies solely in my tenacity." Not fewer hurdles but more jumps are what is needed.

Electrifying Dynamic Desire Releases the Genius Within

In an interview with *Harper's Magazine* in 1890, Thomas Edison said, "I have constructed 3,000 different theories in connection with the electric light.... Yet only in two cases did my experiments prove the truth of my theory."

By that time, Edison had been working on the electric light for over ten years, not including the original research that led him to the bamboo filament in 1880. After focusing on platinum, he turned to carbon, experimenting with cotton threads, as well as various papers, cardboards, and woods, coconut hair, fishing line, vulcanized fiber, cork, and some long-fiber plants prior to going with bamboo. Not owning the vital patents on artificial fibers, which were proving to be superior, Edison searched internationally for a more suitable fibrous plant that would offer more resistance than cotton.

The 10,000 experiments people often refer to when talking about Edison's doggedness in inventing the light bulb, were actually conducted in his quest to develop a rechargeable alkaline storage battery for electric cars and trucks.

To be sure, Edison had his share of critics, detractors, and naysayers in the form of consultants, academics, and other manufacturers, calling his ideas: "sheer nonsense," "foolish," "absurd, predicting final, necessary, and ignominious failure," and "so manifestly absurd as to indicate a positive want of knowledge of the electric circuit and the principles governing the construction and operation of electric machines!"

But given his dynamic desire, will to succeed, and relentless action, Edison didn't care what anyone thought or said in disparaging him. With attitudes and habits like that he was bound to succeed. He said, "Many of life's failures are people who didn't realize how close they were to success when they gave up." Keep going until you succeed; then get a new dynamic desire and go some more, repeating the process.

Robert Friedel and Paul Israel, Edison authorities, spoke of his audacity... "For Edison, the search for a practical incandescent light was a bold, even foolhardy plunge into the unknown guided at first more by over confidence and a few half-baked ideas than by science. To suggest otherwise is to rib the inventive act of its human dimension and thus to miss an understanding of the act itself.

According to the authorized biography, *Edison: His Life and Inventions*, when Walter S. Mallory, a friend and associate asked Edison, "Isn't it a shame that with the tremendous amount of work you have done, you haven't been able to get any results?" Edison turned on Mallory like a flash, and with a smile replied: "Results! Why, man, I have gotten lots of results! I know several thousand things that won't work!" Now *that's* perseverance.

During the time all those failed attempts to get the incandescent light bulb to stay lit and to develop the new battery, any average-thinking person who may have known what Edison was doing probably thought he was crazy, just wasting his time. For instance, people had been trying to invent the light bulb for over 50 years; whatever anyone experimented with simply melted or burned out very quickly.

I imagine myself in those situations. I'm doing a drawing, and some part of it isn't working. It doesn't look right. So I use another approach, then another, and another.... Would I be willing to "experiment" with over 10,000 different approaches to the same challenge?

Now apply that to your own situation. Would you have the dynamic desire, patience, and discipline to persist like Edison did? Would you have the tenacity to go through hundreds, or even thousands, of failures in your quest to achieve success? If not, you don't *really* want it!

So-called luck enters only when we hold the door open for it, even after our arm starts to ache. Wisdom has it that, "Luck happens when opportunity and preparedness meet," and that luck is an acronym for, "Labor Under Correct Knowledge." The more dynamic your desire, the "luckier" you'll be!

Dynamic Desire Creates Super-Sweet Success
"When I left home as a boy to tackle the job of making a living, my mother gave me some good advice...'Milton, you

are now going out into the world to make a man of yourself. My best advice to you is when you tackle a job stick to it until you have mastered it.'

"I never have forgotten those words, and now, when I think of the chocolate business and the way it has grown, I think it was my mother's advice that spurred me on and helped me overcome my obstacles. You can only make money by giving people what they want, and making good use of your opportunities.

"...I started out with the determination to make a better nickel chocolate bar than any of my competitors, and I did so."

After three business failures, including bankruptcy, by the time he was 29, Milton Hershey was broke. But learning well about business from his mistakes, together with hard work and perseverance, this largely uneducated man became the world's largest maker of chocolate. He learned first-hand, and later would say, "Difficulties show men what they are."

While his father, Henry, never became financially successful, he was an imaginative, inquiring, self-assured dreamer who loved books and learning. Even though he failed 17 times he'd say, "Well that happened; let's move on. It's not going to stop me!"

Some of Milton's relatives thought that, like his father, he'd never succeed. But he was inspired by Henry's positive thinking, as well as his tenacity in picking himself back up whenever he failed. Even so, his strict mother, Fanny, daughter of a Mennonite bishop, was weary of Henry's repeated failures and took charge of raising the boy.

In his quest for success, Henry had moved the family so many times that, even though smart, Milton, at 13, had barely finished the fourth grade, the last year of his fragmented schooling. Fanny then decided it would be best that he not go back to school and instead learn a trade. So with Henry wanting the boy to be a journalist, he found him work with a local newspaper.

But like many today Milton hated his job, purposely getting himself fired by throwing his hat into the printing press. Stepping in, his mother helped him get an apprenticeship with a Lancaster confectioner, even though Henry thought it to be a woman's job. After Milton was situated, Fanny and Henry finally separated (they had been at odds for some time), and she and Milton moved into a small house in Lancaster. He not only learned the art of making candy, including caramels, fudge, and peppermints, but also how to oversee employees, buy ingredients, manage inventory, and price products.

Loving the work, he discovered what he wanted to do with his life and began developing dynamic desire. After working there four years, Milton declared, "If I can make money for my employer, why can't I do just as well for myself? I'm going to like being a confectioner, I know I shall!"

So, at 19, he decided to strike out on his own, knowing that in order to succeed he'd have to put his heart and soul into it. Based on her faith, his mother had taught him that wealth achieved by hard work was a sign of God's grace.

Convincing his uncle, Abraham Snavely, to lend him some money to get started, he moved to Philadelphia and on June 1, 1876 opened a candy shop. Anticipating large crowds attending the Centennial Celebration, he thought it would be an opportune time to launch his enterprise. His mother and Aunt Mattie then came to the city to help; his aunt lending him about $3,000 in today's money.

In 1881 Henry also went to help his son. He not only sold Milton's candy, but also designed a unique display cabinet for Milton to market to other candy companies. Henry told Milton…"If you want to make money, you've got to do things in a big way." While Milton started to advertise the cabinet, along with the medicated cough drops formulated by his father, he just didn't have the finances to support another venture.

Working 16-hour days making his "French Secrets" candy, wrapped with a message inside, he also sold other candies, nuts, and ice cream. After seven years Milton's business was generating income, but not enough to pay off debts or make a profit. In addition, the steep, unpredictable sugar costs contributed to the demise of his first business, forcing him into bankruptcy. Years later he would control his own sugar supply by owning and operating plantations and a refinery in Cuba, along with building a railroad to transport his sugar to the docks. He also built rental homes, a general store, a free public school, and recreational facilities for his workers.

Holding on to his dream, and prompted by his father who was working in the booming Denver, Colorado silver mines, Milton went west, taking a job with a local caramel maker. There he discovered a key ingredient to his eventual success, fresh whole milk, which not only made the candy taste better but also extended its shelf life.

After his Denver experience, Milton followed his father to Chicago and made candies for the wholesale trade. But the venture was short-lived, as the candy business there proved too competitive. While his father remained in Chicago working as a business agent, Milton explored New Orleans. Realizing it would be too expensive to move his candy-making equipment there, he returned to Lancaster.

In 1883 he went to New York City and began working for a candy shop to learn about the market, while starting his own business on the side. He then went independent making and selling taffy from his own store; and, once again, his mother and Aunt Mattie came to help.

By summer 1886 he found himself without the funds to keep the business going. So he packed up his equipment and shipped it to Lancaster, while barely having enough money to pay for the three of them to get back home.

As a man of integrity, Milton later shared, "When I failed in New York City I was able to pay my creditors 40 cents on the dollar. As soon as I got on my feet financially I returned to and paid my creditors the remaining 60 percent of my indebtedness. I never did anything since that gave me as much satisfaction as when I paid back that money."

Twenty-nine and broke, Milton's maternal uncles thought he was as irresponsible as they believed his father was, unable to imagine he would ever succeed. But Milton wouldn't give up. Having his father's bounce-back attitude, their rejection only served to spur him on, more determined than ever! Again, Aunt Mattie agreed to lend him some money, enabling him to rent a room and also buy the ingredients, including whole fresh milk to experiment with...before he started making caramels.

When he got to the flavor and texture he liked he started production, calling his candy "Crystal A" caramels. Making them during the day, in the evening he would load them into a pushcart and peddle them on the streets. One of his customers, a candy importer from England, ordered more than $60,000 worth in today's dollars, enabling Milton to get a swing loan from the bank to expand his operation.

Naming his business the Lancaster Caramel Company, in only a few short years his factory grew to occupy a city block, 450,000 square feet, making him one of Lancaster's most outstanding citizens. With the naysayers disproven, no one could deny Milton Hershey's tenacity to succeed. By 1891 he had enough money to buy a large house in Lancaster, remodeling and re-landscaping it to suit.

In 1893 he attended the World's Columbian Exposition in Chicago where he purchased German chocolate-making equipment, shipped it to Lancaster, and began making chocolate coatings for his caramels. Continuing to operate from the Lancaster facility, the following year Milton founded Hershey Chocolate Company, and by 1895 added bars as well as chocolate for drinking and baking.

Realizing caramels were too rich for everyday consumption, he focused on chocolate...believing it would make for a more enduring business. Milton's objective was to mass produce chocolate while making it inexpensive enough so anyone could afford it on a regular basis, selling his bars for five cents! Up until then chocolate had been an expensive luxury for the more affluent.

In 1897 Milton bought back his grandparents' farm, and had his father live there until he passed away in 1904, while he had his mother live with him in Lancaster. Milton would travel to the farm to conduct experiments to create the blend of chocolate he liked.

In 1898 he married Catherine "Kitty" Sweeney, who he met on a sales trip to upstate New York. He soon bought a house in Lancaster for his mother who then moved out of the big house, providing Milton and Kitty with privacy. While they loved children they were unable to have their own.

By 1900, Milton, sensing that the caramel business had peaked, decided to focus on chocolate, and sold the caramel company to competitors for about $20 million in today's dollars. Providing him with all the money he would need for his biggest venture, he started by renting a wing of the caramel factory from the new owner and concentrated on making chocolate.

After deciding against Lancaster because the land was too expensive, Milton conducted a four-state search for the best location to build his factory. Choosing rural Derry Church, PA, his birthplace, in 1902 he began purchasing land (eventually amounting to nearly 10,000 acres), as its extensive dairy farms could provide the fresh whole milk needed for chocolate production. Compared to building in a city, the in-the-middle-of-nowhere location would be an economical area in which to operate and expand his business, as well as for future employees to live.

In early 1903, after Kitty had visited the land that was staked out to indicate the foundation of the factory, she told Milton, "You ought to go and have your head examined!"

Even his business associates thought he was crazy to build in such a remote area. But Milton would not be dissuaded. And even though he hadn't yet developed the best formulation for the mass production of chocolate, he forged ahead knowing it would be developed.

Envisioning what he wanted to accomplish, and with factory construction starting at the end of that winter, Hershey would also build a safe, beautiful, wholesome small town for his workers. It would include houses they could purchase, a school, bank, post office, department store, churches, hospital, public library, gymnasium, parks and gardens, zoo, utilities, quarry, trolley car system for transporting workers from outlaying areas as well as milk from the farms, and later a small airport as well as a community college. While only eight percent of homes in the US had indoor plumbing, electricity, and central heating, all the homes in Hershey were so equipped.

Here's a brief list of some of Milton Hershey's many accomplishments:

* In 1909, at 58, starting with four orphaned boys, Milton and Kitty established the Hershey Industrial School. Six years later Kitty passed away, and Milton carried her photo every day for the rest of his life, never remarrying. Forming the Hershey Trust in 1918, during his lifetime he gave most of his personal wealth to it, with assets today of more than $12 billion! Nearly 2,000 boys and girls are now enrolled in what is known as the Milton Hershey School, the richest private charity for children in the US; the Trust controlling all Hershey enterprises.

* Even though his mother was against it, Milton opened Hershey Park in 1907 as a picnic grove for his employees, relatives, and town residents. After its popularity grew his mother enjoyed strolling the park, now one of the US's top-ten most popular theme parks, admission including free access to Zoo-America.

- Built Hershey's first golf course in 1915, which today has three world-class courses.

- Instituted the US's first profit-sharing plan in 1923.

- Founded Hershey Bears Hockey Club in 1932.It's the oldest member of the American Hockey League.

- Prospering through the Depression, Hershey kept men busy building the magnificent Spanish-style Hotel Hershey, high on a hill overlooking his town, a modern office building, sports arena, stadium, and a huge junior-senior high school. When a foreman told him he had a machine that does the work of 40 men, Milton said to get rid of it and hire the men! In 1930 he gave his mansion to the new Hershey Country Club as a club house, living in two rooms on the second floor until he passed away in October 1945.

- As a world-leading confectioner, Hershey's product line includes such iconic brands as: a variety of Hershey's Kisses, Hershey Bars, Hershey's with Almonds, Mounds, and Almond Joy; Reese's Peanut Butter Cups, Pieces, Whipps, and Take 5; Twizzlers, Kit Kat, Hershey's Extra Dark and Cadbury Bars, Payday, Heath Bars, Whoppers, Milk Duds, and York Peppermint Patties, as well as other high-quality chocolate, confectionery, and beverages.

At 85 Milton was asked at what age he believed a man was at his best: "That's a difficult question to answer. Some men are washed up when they are forty, while others just get started at that age. The other day I was shown an old newspaper clipping about myself which explained why I had founded the school for orphan boys. The headline read, 'Hershey Feels the End Is Near.' Twenty-five years have passed since then, and in those years I have been able to accomplish many of the things I wanted to do. That doesn't look as though I sat down and waited for the end, does it?"

When asked about his perspective on aging and success, Hershey said, "Of course there are exceptions, but an interest in something new triumphs over the calendar. Since I turned 70…I've started dozens of new enterprises. Now at 85 I'm engaged in the greatest enterprise of all… [helping our troops in World War II by producing millions of non-melting US Army Field Ration D bars]."

His dedication to mass-producing chocolate affordable by the masses, coupled with a deep sense of moral commitment and generosity was exemplified by how he conducted his businesses, built his town, and left his fortune to his school. It all led to one of the greatest legacies in history that continues benefiting people the world over.

As Milton shared…"A man accomplishes little when he thinks and acts alone, and is only happy in proportion as he makes others feel happy…. Some people think that I've had an easy time of it. They say I have the Hershey luck, whatever that is, and as a result money flowed into my lap. But luck had nothing to do with my success…my success is the result of not being satisfied with mediocrity, and in making the most of my opportunities."

Since his death at 88, as a businessman and philanthropist, Milton Hershey's dynamic desire led to an ongoing legacy of making a difference. In 1963 (the same year Hershey Kiss-shaped street lamps were erected along Chocolate Avenue!) offering a gift, in today's dollars, of nearly $400 million from the Milton S. Hershey Foundation, The Penn State Milton S. Hershey Medical Center was founded. This world-class, multi-award winning facility includes a top-ranking teaching hospital, 475-bed general medical and surgical facility, children's hospital, and research facilities.

Often referred to as "the Henry Ford of chocolate makers," Milton Hershey was, nevertheless, thankful and reserved; running his business with his heart…and his people loved him. Unlike other business giants of his day, he had a calm demeanor and was never pretentious. He built his home in the community he built and loved, situated with a view of the factory.

Now ask yourself…"What if Milton Hershey had quit when his first, second, or third business failed?" But more importantly, ask yourself…"What would happen if I were to quit after the first, second, or third time I endeavored to accomplish something worthwhile?" There's no way you could ever succeed! Would that be acceptable to you?

When You Fail, Learn All You Can from It…*and Keep Pressing on Toward Your Goal!*

British playwright J.M. Barrie wrote, "We are all of us failures—at least, the best of us are." Barrie understood the positive role failure can play in our lives. Edison certainly knew he had one of the highest failure rates ever. But he considered failure as a powerful learning tool when properly utilized. Today, his name is synonymous with the words "genius" and "success."

Defeat provides the best homework assignments. Failure is always part of the picture. You can't avoid it. Our education consists largely of learning what won't work. Think about it. The more you're willing to fail, the greater your chance for success. Like all great people, Edison literally failed his way to success, and you can too. Don't ever be afraid to fail; it's simply part and parcel of succeeding.

While feelings of futility are, at times, inevitable, remember, they're just feelings. They'll pass when we learn to weather them with faith. Successful people awaken to days of dark moods but they get out of bed and get moving anyway. In the final analysis, people who ultimately fail curl into a fetal position and pull the blanket of futility over their heads.

The Japanese have a wonderful proverb: "Fall seven times, stand up eight." Successful people are simply people who formerly failed, have a stubborn, persistent dynamic desire, and an undying belief in themselves and the value of what they're doing.

We need to be more like children in our quest to succeed. Kids make mistakes and generally take it in stride. At some level, they understand that it's only a part of their learning. Did you color inside the lines the first time you picked up a crayon? Did you stay upright on your bicycle the day your training wheels were taken off?

Be more childlike in your approach to life. Don't mind falling now and then. Better to fall on your backside than to just sit on it and not strive to reach your goals and dreams!

The fear of looking foolish is a foolish way to look at yourself. Every face, seen in the right light, has traces of egg on it. Keep a playful perspective on all things, and you'll always have plenty of shelf-space in your medicine cabinet.

Laugh and the world laughs with you. Cry and your mascara runs, or your cheeks get wet. A sense of humor is available to everyone to use in dealing with the challenges of life, while not taking ourselves too seriously. Feel free to cultivate and use it.

"*If I can make money for my employer, why can't I do just as well for myself?*"

[Then some years after he had achieved success he said...]

"*When I left home as a boy to tackle the job of making a living, my mother gave me some good advice...*

"*'Milton, you are now going out into the world to make a man of yourself. My best advice to you is when you tackle a job stick to it until you have mastered it.'*

"*I never have forgotten those words, and now, when I think of the chocolate business and the way it has grown, I think it was my mother's advice that spurred me on and helped me overcome my obstacles.*

"*You can only make money by giving people what they want, and making good use of your opportunities.*"

—Milton S. Hershey

Epilogue
Yes, Your Desire IS Your GIFT!

*"...intense desire creates not only its own opportunities,
but also its own talents."*   —Eric Hoffer

When you sincerely want success—and apply yourself—you can have it. It's easier said than done, of course, but then *everything* is easier said than done. So what? Just go do it!

Take, for example, my father-in-law. He never went beyond the tenth grade. It was during the Depression, and he quit school to find work so he could help his family. After serving in World War II, he came home to a blue-collar factory job. The money wasn't good.

As the years passed, the money never became good, but he still managed to pay off a mortgage and support a family, even though he never liked his job. But while his coworkers met after hours at a local bar to hoist a few and complain about their lot in life, my father-in-law studied books on carpentry, plumbing, and electricity—filling his head with practical knowledge. He had developed the dynamic desire to go into business for himself, doing whatever it took to make it happen. Desire was his gift.

He remembered the day he retired from his factory job. After work, he drop-kicked his lunch pail down the street. For the rest of his life, he had all the business he could handle. His phone was always ringing with jobs to be done. His practical skills, self-taught, kept him in demand—and making good money.

People often ask the question, "How can I get motivated and stay motivated?" To me, that's like asking, "How do I get dressed in the morning? How do I brush my teeth? How do I keep from starving to death?" *You* take responsibility for all these things; you've made them habits that you don't even have to think about. You just automatically do them!

No one else but you can give you a sustaining belief in yourself or the ongoing desire to achieve. No one but you can act on that desire. Just like my father-in-law, the power of developing dynamic desire will enable you to achieve your desire. Remember, your desire IS your gift! It will help you create the discipline and sustain the perseverance needed to reach your dreams and goals...

I'll tell you something that helps many people stay motivated, and it'll help you too. Talk to your leader or mentor. Ask for a recommended reading list of positive books. Read from one of them at least 15-20 minutes a day. Great times to do this are during your early morning alone time, at coffee or lunch breaks at work, and right before you turn the light out to go to sleep.

Also, as suggested before, ask your leader or mentor for a list of recommended continuing education audios. Listen to them as you get ready for the day, while in your vehicle and preparing for bed. Listen to these recordings again and again. People who win are on a constant quest for knowledge, and keep themselves motivated by focusing on their goals and dreams and listening to inspiring, upbeat music and speakers.

Shared knowledge of universal truths forms the broadest brotherhood, spanning both space and time. We think of the great men and women of history as having been larger than life, but they were no larger than you and I. They suffered the same doubts, frustrations, and setbacks we all face... and much, much more. We have a lot to learn from them about life, the power of developing dynamic desire, and how to achieve and sustain the journey of success.

Samuel Johnson, the 18th Century writer, said, "Life, though it be short, is made shorter by waste of time." Based on insurance company actuarial tables, I have only 1,000 weeks left to live. But if the insurance companies are wrong for me, and I see my 100th birthday, I have about 2,200 more weeks to live. That fact helps me stay focused!

Life is a wonderful function to which everyone is invited, but most have either failed to ask for directions to it or else copied down the wrong address. Don't be one of them.

I truly admire the late Steve Allen, who I had the opportunity to meet and speak with some years ago. He used time more efficiently than anyone else I know. To function well he needed 10 to 12 hours of sleep, but learned how to maximize his productivity while awake.

The author of 53 books, he dictated them into small recorders he kept in his pocket, on the nightstand by his bed, and in his car. He was the composer of more than 5,000 songs, which placed him in the *Guinness Book of World Records*. When he wasn't writing jokes, he stayed busy with a full schedule of concert and nightclub appearances.

At 78, Steve Allen continued to think creatively and productively. His final performance was given the night before he died—to a sold-out house.

He liked to say, "We should all die with our desks left cluttered with tasks yet to be done." His life was dedicated to the fulfillment of his dreams and desires. His pursuing them brought meaning, vitality, and joy to all of his days.

Death is Nature's way of reminding us to be productive! Enjoy but never settle for what and where you are. Always strive to accomplish even bigger dreams. Remember, success is found in the journey. Being complacent and resting on your laurels is often an indication that you haven't developed enough dynamic desire to sustain and drive you forward. If that's the case, discover a new dream, a new desire, something that you're passionate about achieving that will give your life new meaning, new verve, and a new zest!

The first step to a continuously successful life is to realize that everything you need for success is already within you—you were born with it. Motivational speakers and authors can and do inspire us, but the only "motivational speaker" who can move *you* into action is *you*! Motivation is not an external flame. It's found deep inside, and you need to light and stoke its fire every day. Your attitude either fuels or smothers it.

So speak your desire to *yourself* and get moving. That's where you'll find your power. As Sir Isaac Newton's First Law of Motion states, "...a body in motion tends to stay in motion..."

What do you most desire in life? That's your gift; that's what drives you. Act on it with faith, discipline, and perseverance and, in time, you will be successful. If I can do it with art, you can achieve your dream, too, in whatever area of endeavor you may choose.

Commit to and forge ahead as you work toward reaching your potential by developing dynamic desire. Take appropriate action every day, and your gifts and talents will flourish. Discover, cultivate, increase, and sustain the lifeblood of all success.

"*So what's your greatest desire ...now that you know it's your special gift? Embrace it and dynamically develop it with the commitment to make it happen. Act on it with relentless unwavering discipline and perseverance.*

"Do whatever it takes and you can create the richer, happier, more meaningful life you've been longing for...and even beyond!"

—The Publisher

Who Is Bruce Garrabrandt?

Bruce Garrabrandt is a popular and sought after professional artist, writer, and inspiring motivational speaker. With his wife, Jan, he is also innkeeper of *The Artist's Inn & Gallery*, a bed and breakfast, as well as The Olde Stone Cottage, both nestled in the beautiful Pennsylvania Dutch Country of Lancaster County.